Curriculum Development and Evaluation

A Design for Improvement

Jerry J. Bellon
Janet R. Handler
The University of Tennessee

D1373437

**KENDALL/HUNT
PUBLISHING COMPANY**
Dubuque, Iowa

LB
1570
.B398
1982

B   402720   01

Contents

Preface

    We feel this book can make a unique contribution to those interested in developing and improving educational programs. In this book development and evaluation are presented as simultaneous, complementary processes. We know that this approach to improvement is very practical and usable. It is based on extensive field experience with school systems throughout the United States. Many of the educational leaders we have worked with have expressed the need for a resource book that would help guide their program improvement activities. The processes we have described in the book have been used with a wide variety of school systems. The approaches used to improve programs in large urban systems have been found to be equally successful with small suburban and rural systems. We know that these generic development and evaluation processes can be applied to most school settings.

    In addition to educators in the field, students in curriculum classes should find this book to be a helpful resource. The leading curriculum and evaluation theorists have been referenced and their concepts related to the design that we have developed. We have used the first drafts of this material with several graduate and undergraduate curriculum classes. The feedback from these students has been helpful in refining and clarifying the basic concepts. Their enthusiastic response has been most rewarding and has given additional support to this publication effort.

    After the introductory chapter, the book follows a format that should help the reader understand how to develop a plan for program improvement. Basic concepts and definitions are presented in the first section of each chapter. These are followed by propositions that give direction to instructional improvement activities. The propositions have emerged from both theory and successful practice.

    The designs for analysis include suggested questions as well as possible data collection activities. Alternative approaches to curriculum development and evaluation are suggested in the design procedures. Each of the design sections is followed by a comparative summary of related models and frameworks. The bibliographies contain references that will assist the reader in developing a solid curriculum development and evaluation information base.

    The development and renewal activities at the end of each chapter can be especially helpful to those interested in improving their skills, competencies, and understanding of the processes and concepts presented in this book. The readings suggested in these activities are considered to be most important for improving and clarifying knowledge about approaches to program improvement. The development and renewal activities can serve as an excellent point of departure for those committed to personal and professional renewal.

    It should be pointed out that this book is closely related to two books that deal with instructional improvement. *Classroom Supervision and Instructional Improvement* by Bellon and Bellon (Kendall/Hunt, 1982) focuses on a supervision and observation program aimed at improving teaching and learning. *Instructional Improvement: Principles and Processes* by Bellon, Bellon, and Handler (Kendall/Hunt, 1977) provides an information base for improving classroom instruction. The three books should be especially helpful to those who are initiating programs to improve curriculum, instruction, and student learning.

Several people have been most helpful in the preparation of the manuscript. Walter Celusta has assisted with the research and the preparation of the bibliographic material. He has also carefully reviewed and critiqued each chapter. Elner Bellon reviewed the manuscript and offered a number of valuable suggestions that helped clarify the material. She also invested considerable time and energy doing the final proof reading.

Mary Waggoner, Dorothy McCullough and Faye Benjamin were responsible for the manuscript preparation. Their willingness to spend many extra hours typing and preparing each draft made it possible for us to complete this project.

J.J.B.
J.R.H.

Chapter 1

Curriculum Development and Evaluation: A Gradual Synthesis

Introduction

Concepts and processes of curriculum development and evaluation have undergone many important changes since the beginning of public education in the United States. Prior to 1900, the primary focus of educational activity was on broadening the availability of public education, determining the subjects to be taught, and attempting to train teachers to use improved methods of presentation.

Formal systematic curriculum development and evaluation activities did not exist during the early expansion of public education. In the twentieth century, particularly since the 1930's, curriculum development and evaluation have received increased attention. Although development and evaluation have generally been treated as separate fields of study with limited interaction, a careful analysis reveals many common influences, activities, and trends. Curriculum development and evaluation theorists and practitioners have been affected by similar social, political, and economic forces. Important changes in development and evaluation approaches appear to have been influenced by changes in leadership theory and practice. The following sections provide a brief overview of major events in curriculum development and evaluation. The position has been taken that when curriculum development and evaluation are seen as simultaneous, interactive processes educational programs can be improved. When programs are improved, the educational expectations of a school or district are more likely to be achieved.

Early Efforts: Measurement and Scientific Models Take Precedence

Prior to the 1930's several events took place which would have a significant influence on future curriculum development and evaluation activities. The Commission on the Reorganization of Secondary Education issued a report in 1918 delineating three bases of curriculum development that were to have a significant influence on future curriculum activities. These bases were: the society, the student population, and educational theory and practice. The Commission's seven general goals for secondary education were more widely popularized. They were known as the Cardinal Principles and emphasized concern for: health, command of fundamental processes, worthy home membership, vocation, citizenship, worthy use of leisure time, and ethical character. By setting forth these broad statements of direction, curriculum developers were provided with generally accepted purposes to guide planning and evaluation activities.

In a less well known development during this period, the basis for specifying behavioral objectives was also established. A number of educators were attempting to apply the results of child development studies to modify the organization and placement of subject matter. Superintendent Carleton Washburne of Winnetka, Illinois, advanced these efforts by initiating the use of self instructional materials as part of an individualized instruction program. These self corrective units were devised to promote mastery of specified learning outcomes, an idea that has once again become popular. The Winnetka program represented the first systemwide attempt to tailor the curriculum to meet individual student needs. Washburne's efforts were also influential in the development of textbooks geared to student performance levels.

These early developments were supported by changes in the field of psychology. There was a shift away from the "faculty psychology" emphasis on mental discipline and transfer of learning. Beginning with Thorndike's classic studies, educators and experimental psychologists initiated intensive studies of intelligence, performance, and thinking processes. A wide variety of standardized tests were developed to determine how well students could perform a range of educational tasks. Supporters of both the subject matter oriented and child or experience centered approaches to curriculum were actively involved in the development and application of various quantitative instruments to measure the effects of their curricula.

The need to devise tools for measuring qualitative outcomes was often expressed but not fulfilled during this period. However, the quantitative study of educational outcomes was actively pursued and received added impetus during and after World War I. A great deal of publicity was generated by the performance of recruits on tests given during induction to the armed services. The standardized, or norm referenced, tests developed and refined during the 1920's have led to the frequent characterization of this period as the era of mental measurement.

It has been noted by such authorities as Oscar Buros (1977) that in many ways measurement reached its peak in terms of both emphasis and excellence during the late 1920's and early 1930's. Until the mid to late 1930's educational evaluation was popularly equated with these measurement activities. The formula $E=M$, or evaluation is identical to measurement, has been used to represent this early measurement approach to evaluation.

The measurement orientation of this period can also be seen in early curriculum planning frameworks proposed by Bobbitt, Charters, and others. This scientific study of the curriculum was influenced by paradigms adapted from industrial models that emphasized job or activity analysis, utilitarian as well as traditional subjects, and standardized testing to determine effectiveness of training or instruction.

Franklin Bobbitt and W. W. Charters were leading proponents of activity or job analysis. In this approach, the curriculum developer's major task was seen as delineating the important areas of adult endeavor and gradually breaking these down into small teachable segments. In their writings, Bobbitt (1918) and Charters (1923) stressed the school's role in preparing learners for adult life. However, since standardized tests were widely used during this period, there were frequent and serious discrepancies between learning expectations and the measures used to assess performance.

Adoption of the bureaucratic or line and staff model of educational leadership was another example of industry's influence on curriculum activity. Planning committees chosen and dominated by administrators became the school districts' major approach to developing or revising courses of study or other curriculum materials. This approach is still used by some educational systems, although with less frequency in recent years.

Broadening the Measurement Concept:
The Start of Rational Curriculum Planning

A number of important events took place during the decades prior to the mid 1930's which set the stage for several influential educational trends. However, very little impact was made on curriculum development and evaluation until the Eight Year Study (1933–1941) was initiated. This project was to have a significant influence on curriculum development and evaluation concepts and applications.

The Eight Year Study was conducted to determine the effects of high school curriculum revisions, made possible by waivers of college entrance requirements, on students' success in college. Findings of this longitudinal study provided needed support for curriculum experimentation efforts. Of great consequence was the work done by Ralph Tyler as head of the study's evaluation committee. While the start of World War II and the period of conservatism which followed the war interfered with action on the research results, Tyler's activities helped establish a set of specific guidelines for goal based evaluation.

Tyler's efforts resulted in a widely accepted definition of evaluation as the degree of congruence or match between performance and objectives. The definition, symbolized by the formula $E = (P \cong O)$, has been a persistent influence on evaluation theory and practice. Tyler's work provided a basis for such significant developments of later years as criterion referenced measurement and competency based instructional programs.

Although there were a number of important changes taking place in education during the 1940's and 1950's, few events stand out as having a special impact on curriculum or evaluation activities. Curriculum development publications by Ralph Tyler were perhaps the most significant activities of this era. Tyler's approach to deriving educational goals and objectives was based on several important factors. They included: philosophy, psychology, and the classic referent points of students, society, and subject matter. His formulation of four guiding questions became widely known as the framework for rational curriculum development. These questions dealt with: setting forth the objectives to be attained, determining the types of learning experiences to be provided, deciding how these should be organized, and thinking ahead to ways in which the achievement of objectives would be measured. The inclusion of the fourth question added an important evaluative dimension to the curriculum planning process. This rather straight forward and simple question represented a major conceptual breakthrough in curriculum development and evaluation. Tyler's rational approach, presented in his 1949 book, has since been strengthened by Taba, Goodlad, and other curriculum leaders. It has had a considerable influence on the curriculum field, yet has been the subject of some controversy during the decades of rapid change that followed the rather quiet postwar period in education.

Beginning of the Modern Era: Development and Evaluation
Emerge as Major Areas of the Curriculum Field

The years following 1957 have come to be known by many educators as the post Sputnik era. The Soviet Union's achievements in the space race with the United States had a tremendous impact on American education. A large number of curriculum development projects were instituted during the late 1950's and early 1960's which were the result of an intense national interest in curricular reform. Subject matter specialists, often supported by substantial federal grants, mobilized to develop the types of curriculum materials that they believed would promote academic excellence, especially in science and mathematics.

Curriculum development processes during this period tended to emphasize the movement of content downward to lower grades. Subject specialists advocated the use in text materials of the precise language and ways of thinking preferred by practitioners of the various academic specialties. Organizing curriculum content according to the structure of each discipline was among the influential ideas popularized by Jerome Bruner (1960), a psychologist whose work was highly regarded by developers of national curriculum projects. These projects included the subject fields of mathematics, physics, biology, and chemistry. Developers of these academic projects made use of field testing and other research and development (R & D) concepts. However, they were often unable to make the content and organization of their materials sufficiently accessible to teachers and students who were the intended recipients of the program. While influential at the time, the long term effects of the national curriculum projects have been difficult to assess. Drawing strong criticism as well as support in recent years, these projects are believed by many to have contributed to the emergence of a "back to the basics" movement during the late 1970's and early 1980's.

The work by Benjamin Bloom (1956) and several colleagues in formulating and refining taxonomies of educational objectives was an important parallel development of this period of rapid change. Analysis of cognitive, affective, and psychomotor outcomes became a focal point for curricular and instructional activity. Robert Mager's work in the area of behavioral objectives also gained national attention during the 1960's. Teachers were urged to write detailed objectives for their lessons which included: expected behaviors, background conditions, success criteria, and time frames. The emphasis placed on detailed specification of behavioral outcomes increased the precision of some curriculum activities, but led to negative consequences as well. Focusing on lower level cognitive outcomes, relying on limited measuring strategies, and utilizing inflexible or arbitrary success criteria were among the drawbacks that have been cited. The behavioral objectives movement did foster an interest in measuring program success in relation to specific learning objectives. This interest was reflected in the rise of competency based programs, criterion referenced measures, proficiency tests, and objectives based curricula. It also influenced the design of the National Assessment of Educational Progress, a large scale testing program which exemplified the growing interest in a precise determination of student learning.

A great deal of Tyler's early work in evaluation, focusing particularly on matching performance to objectives, became evident in the new developments. Hilda Taba's publication in 1962 gave further impetus to the rational approach advocated by Tyler. Diagnosis of needs and inclusion of evaluation activities as part of the curriculum development process became much more widely accepted as a result of Taba's work.

The concept of evaluation was advanced considerably about this time by several important publications. Lee Cronbach's 1963 paper, "Course Improvement Through Evaluation," clarified and strengthened the position that evaluation is an integral part of curriculum development and must not be treated as merely an appendage. Cronbach also argued for a broader description of program outcomes rather than narrow definitions of the scope of evaluation activity. This theme was later developed by Robert Stake and Michael Scriven in their influential writings on evaluation.

Scriven's early work, including a 1967 paper entitled "The Methodology of Evaluation," helped firmly establish him as a leading thinker and catalyst in the field. Scriven urged evaluators to carefully analyze and distinguish between the goals or purposes of evaluation and the roles it can fulfill in education. Scriven continues to be one of the most influential individuals associated with evaluation today. His contributions include: the concepts of formative and summative evaluation, the distinction between pay-off and intrinsic evaluation, the process of evaluating goals to determine their worth, the concept of meta evaluation, and the goal-free evaluation approach.

It was fortunate that the work of Cronbach and Scriven coincided with the extensive federal funding of educational programs. The Elementary and Secondary Education Act (ESEA) and the Vocational Education Act were large and influential programs established during this period. They gave state and local agencies considerable responsibility for managing the funds provided. Legislators came to recognize the importance of holding these agencies accountable for providing evidence that intended results were being achieved. The time was right for expanding assessment and evaluation processes and concepts.

Curriculum Development and Evaluation in the Modern Era: State of the Art

As the 1960's drew to a close and the 1970's began, several distinct currents were evident in the curriculum field. Proponents of specific behavioral objectives were moving ahead with technological curriculum building efforts, using programmed units, modules, and often sophisticated new equipment.

Advocates of humanistic approaches, such as Maslow, Rogers, Eisner, and Combs, were at the same time encouraging greater attention to personal needs, interests, and values in the curriculum. Eisner's "expressive objectives" (1969) were among their few concessions to the notion of specified learning outcomes, and these may emerge largely during or after some worthwhile activity. The curriculum development approach taken by the humanistic theorists may perhaps be most closely approximated by the interpersonal relations model suggested by Carl Rogers in 1967 (Zais, 1976). Sensitivity group experiences and other encounter techniques were utilized in this approach to bring together various participants for brainstorming and discussion purposes.

A new way of thinking about the concept of evaluation emerged during the period of growing humanistic concern. The view that evaluation is equivalent to professional judgment concerning worth or value, symbolically represented as $E = PJ$, gained widespread interest at this time.

One of the best known of several important evaluation paradigms or frameworks exemplifies the judgmental focus. Robert Stake's evaluation framework establishes a data matrix in which information about antecedents (background conditions), transactions (ongoing events), and outcomes is examined. Judgments are made concerning how well observed occurrences correspond with intents of the program developers. The concept of responsive evaluation developed in Stake's recent writing expands the notion of professional judgment and emphasizes the need for human sensitivity in evaluative processes (Stake, 1976). This idea is also favored by Eisner (1979), in his advocacy of educational "connisseurship," and by those supporting naturalistic, observation based approaches to evaluation. These theorists and others who share their views have considerably advanced the professional judgment concept beyond the era when accreditation activities served as the most widespread example of this evaluation approach. Their ideas have helped those concerned with curriculum improvement probe the more complex and often subtle workings and results of educational programs.

The development of new frameworks has also been a concern of another group of evaluation specialists. These individuals regard evaluation as a process of determining the extent to which goals have been attained. Recent work by Tyler, Popham, and Hammond has contributed to the refinement of goal referenced evaluation processes. Advances in criterion or domain referenced testing have accompanied the effort to improve development and evaluation practice. Evaluators favoring this approach are becoming more aware of the need to identify appropriate measures for goals outside the realm of cognitive learning outcomes. Clear delineation of major goals or expectations is another important prerequisite for effective goal referenced evaluation. Steps may be taken during the development and evaluation process itself to be sure that all important goals are identified.

An interest in systems approaches, which have provisions for feedback and correction built into their designs, has been supported by several prominent curriculum development leaders. Saylor and Alexander, MacDonald, and Joyce are curriculum leaders who support systematic development processes.

A corresponding concern for systems oriented paradigms has the support of a number of evaluation specialists. Stufflebeam and Provus viewed evaluation as a process for aiding decision makers by providing pertinent and timely information. They have developed complex evaluation frameworks which are designed to generate information for decision making. Stufflebeam's widely known model (CIPP), adopted and popularized by Phi Delta Kappa for program evaluation, requires systematic decision making throughout four distinct phases or types of evaluation: context, input, process, and product. The Provus discrepancy model utilizes a detailed series of questions and decision points which reflect considerable management theory influence. When discrepancies are identified between performance and established standards, decisions about appropriate action are made before proceeding further in the evaluation cycle.

The close of the 1970's saw a number of alternative development and evaluation approaches emerge and be applied to various programs. Concern about declining test scores has led a number of people to search for more accurate processes to determine the effects of educational programs. It has also become common for parents and community members to seek greater involvement in curriculum decisions, including assessment of program merit. Legislators have increased their influence on educational activities. Declining enrollments and limited resources have made planning and accountability especially important aspects of all new development and evaluation proposals.

Transactional models and jury or adversary approaches to evaluation represent the most recent group of emerging frameworks. They reflect the spirit of this competitive, negotiation oriented era. Systems such as Program Planning and Budgeting System (PPBS), used by management specialists for planning and resource allocation, have also had a decided influence on recent development and evaluation activities.

As Scriven and several of his colleagues have pointed out, it is probably time for a greater focus on synthesis and application of existing models and frameworks. Curriculum development and evaluation workers need to be encouraged to test their preferred theoretical approaches in a wide range of educational settings. The result of this emphasis on application will be a valuable base of information for further refinement and reassessment of current development and evaluation paradigms.

Expanded application of development and evaluation frameworks will have another important benefit for the field. More and more people at all levels of the educational system will become aware of the need for systematic curriculum development and evaluation. Wise allocation of resources and attention to high priority programs should be important outcomes of these efforts.

Development and Renewal Activities

1. Select one or more references from the Bibliography for additional reading about key trends and events related to curriculum development and evaluation. For any 10 year period of your choice, identify events which occurred, or failed to occur, that seem to contain lessons for those concerned with improving curriculum processes today. Meet with others to discuss the implications of trends or events you have noted.

2. Develop a list of several current developments affecting educational programs locally or nationally. Trace the history or background influences leading to these developments as far back as you can, using reference books or articles as needed.

3. Speak with colleagues or other appropriate individuals concerning their experiences in education during prior curriculum development and evaluation "eras." Before conducting these informal interviews, prepare a set of questions you would like to have answered. If possible, get multiple responses to your questions and compare the different perspectives.

4. Different ways of approaching evaluation have been discussed in this chapter. They include the approaches represented by $E = M$, $E = (P \cong O)$, and $E = PJ$. Systematic evaluation frameworks and other strategies have also been noted. Use the Annotated Bibliography to help you begin to do further reading in this area. Note, as you read, the features of each approach which you find particularly appealing or helpful.

Bibliography

Bloom, Benjamin, et al. *Handbook I: Cognitive Domain.* New York: David McKay Company, Inc., 1956.

Bloom, Benjamin, David R. Krathwohl, and Bertram B. Masia. *Handbook II: Affective Domain.* New York: David McKay Company, Inc., 1956.

Bobbitt, Franklin. *The Curriculum.* Boston: Houghton Mifflin Company, 1918.

Bruner, Jerome S. *The Process of Education.* Cambridge, Mass.: Harvard University Press, 1960.

Buros, Oscar K. "Fifty Years in Testing: Some Reminiscences, Criticisms, and Suggestions." *Educational Researcher,* July-August 1977, pp. 9–15.

Charters, W. W. *Curriculum Construction.* New York: The MacMillan Company, 1923.

Cronbach, L. J. "Course Improvement through Evaluation." *Teachers College Record.* 64, 1963, pp. 672–83.

Doll, Ronald C. *Curriculum Improvement: Decision Making and Process* (3rd ed.) Boston: Allyn and Bacon, Inc., 1974.

Eisner, Elliot W. "Instructional and Expressive Objectives: Their Formulation and Use in Curriculum." In W. J. Popham et. al., *Instructional Objectives,* AERA Monograph No. 3. Chicago: Rand McNally & Co., 1969, pp. 1–18.

———. *The Educational Imagination.* New York: MacMillan Publishing Corp., 1979.

Goodlad, John I. *Curriculum Inquiry: The Study of Curriculum Practice.* New York: McGraw-Hill Book Co., 1979.

Mager, Robert F. *Preparing Instructional Objectives.* Palo Alto, Calif.: Fearon Publishers, 1962.

Smith, B. Othaniel, William O. Stanley, and Harlan J. Shores. *Fundamentals of Curriculum Development.* (Rev. ed.) New York: Harcourt, Brace, & World, Inc., 1957.

Stake, Robert E. *Evaluating the Arts in Education.* Columbus: Charles E. Merrill Publishing Company, 1975.

Taba, Hilda. *Curriculum Development: Theory and Practice.* New York: Harcourt, Brace & World, Inc., 1962.

Tanner, Daniel and Lauren N. Tanner. *Curriculum Development: Theory Into Practice* (2nd ed.) New York: MacMillan Publishing Co., Inc., 1980.

Tyler, Ralph W. *Basic Principles of Curriculum and Instruction.* Chicago: University of Chicago Press, 1949.

Zais, Robert S. *Curriculum: Principles and Foundations.* New York: Thomas Y. Crowell Co., 1976.

Annotated Bibliography of Evaluation References

Popham, W. James. *Educational Evaluation.* Englewood Cliffs, N.J.: Prentice-Hall, Inc., 1975. This is a formal textbook on educational evaluation. The reader is exposed to a number of evaluation models and guidelines. This instructional volume is filled with educational examples which would be helpful in the conduct of educational evaluations.

Saylor, J. Galen and William M. Alexander. *Planning for Better Teaching and Learning,* New York: Holt, Rinehart, and Winston, 1981. An excellent guide for planning and evaluating the curriculum for any educational program. It is comprehensive in its treatment, presenting models of the process of planning and analyzing the factors and steps involved.

Worthen, Blaine R. and James K. Sanders. *Educational Evaluation: Theory and Practice,* Worthington, Ohio: Charles A. Jones Publishing Co., 1973. The authors present models and thinking of many leading evaluation practitioners and theoreticians. It provides the most promising conceptual frameworks proposed for educational evaluations and practical considerations in conducting such evaluations.

Chapter 2

A Systematic Approach to Improvement

Introduction

As the historical overview presented in Chapter 1 illustrated, it has taken many years for a close relationship between curriculum development and evaluation to emerge and gain acceptance. Even today, there are a number of curriculum workers who continue to approach development and evaluation as distinct or unrelated activities. The organizational structure of schools or districts often contributes to this unfortunate separation. In many educational organizations, evaluation and research specialists are located in one department while curriculum development personnel are housed elsewhere. The functions or activities of the two groups may show very little relationship when they are viewed as distinctly separate entities.

Curriculum development activities conducted in the absence of evaluation information are less likely to achieve satisfactory results. Evaluation processes that fail to generate pertinent and timely data for curriculum improvement seem to be similarly shortsighted. An important purpose of this book is to assist curriculum workers at various levels to unify program development and evaluation activities and still capitalize on the benefits of each activity. In this chapter, an overall design for improving educational programs is introduced. The major assumptions underlying the design are also set forth to clarify the rationale for curriculum development and evaluation. Chapters 3 through 7, building on this overview, contain detailed explanations of each component of the design. The frame of reference established in this chapter should serve as a useful departure point for the study of systematic curriculum improvement.

There are several important assumptions which should be noted in interpreting and analyzing the design presented in this book. The statements that follow represent deeply rooted views whose influence will be apparent as the practice of curriculum development and evaluation is discussed. It is assumed that:

1. **The primary purpose of curriculum development and evaluation is to strengthen educational programs so that students will have improved learning opportunities.** Steps being considered for modifying the curriculum need to be assessed in terms of their likely impact on student learning. Although such factors as efficiency, tradition, and special interest groups may influence curriculum decisions, they should be assigned lower priority. By focusing on student learning opportunities, development and evaluation can be carried out as positive future oriented processes. Reactive, backward looking, or highly politicized curriculum activities have no place in schools or districts committed to promoting successful student learning. Although an element of threat or uncertainty may be associated with any evaluation situation, when decisions are based on program quality and learning outcomes the potentially negative aspects of curriculum improvement efforts can be minimized.

2. **Program improvement activities are most effective when personnel at all levels demonstrate a commitment to achieving agreed upon goals.** Educational goals are statements of purpose which lend direction to the curriculum. Program improvement efforts are more likely to be accomplished when all appropriate personnel, including school system

leaders, are actively involved in steps to achieve priority goals. Similarly, each phase of the improvement process should include specific reference to important, agreed upon educational outcomes. When the commitment to achieving worthwhile goals is present, curriculum workers are in an excellent position to demonstrate accountability in its most positive sense.

3. **Curriculum workers at the system or building levels want their educational programs to be well planned and effective.** There are some who feel that teachers and administrators in certain schools or districts are not really interested in curriculum improvement nor willing to make the effort to improve programs. Negative assumptions will not foster improvement efforts. Teachers, administrators, and other curriculum workers do share a desire to be seen as professionally competent. In order to better achieve the conditions that motivate excellent performance, it is important to enable people to work within the context of a well organized, smoothly functioning program. When school system personnel are given clear information about the curriculum improvement process, they will make a commitment to curriculum development and evaluation activities.

4. **Curriculum improvement must be approached as an ongoing systematic process.** While disjointed or piecemeal efforts have often succeeded in bringing about minor improvements, little can be gained from sporadic, poorly planned improvement activities. With the number of subject areas, special projects, and educational services that are now part of most school programs, a systematic approach that allows for feedback and adjustment is crucial. Long range planning which provides frequent opportunities for productive staff involvement will make it possible to bring about desired changes gradually and smoothly. Further, a systematic ongoing process helps ensure that programs remain responsive as the needs of students and communities change.

A Systematic Development and Evaluation Process

If curriculum improvement is to function in the manner implied by these assumptions, development and evaluation need to proceed as simultaneous activities. The activities should be purposeful, well organized and adapted to local conditions. Results should be clearly communicated to all appropriate groups, along with plans for acting on major recommendations.

A framework has been developed to help clarify the curriculum development and evaluation relationships discussed in this book. A schematic representation of the framework is presented in Figure 1.

The principal elements of this framework are: the four areas of focus, the status descriptions, the analysis activities, and the cumulative improvement components. Arrows indicate interaction between elements of the total process. Each element in the design may be improved or adjusted based on information generated by activities in other elements.

The Four Areas of Focus

There are four major areas which receive in depth attention in this process. These are: goals, organization, operations, and outcomes. Although close relationships exist among them, the four areas are sufficiently distinct to be discussed and analyzed separately.

The first area, Goals, deals with the desired outcomes and expectations of the program. Educational goals are general statements of purpose which give direction to the curriculum. Guidelines for developing and assessing goals are presented in Chapter 4 of this book. In order to more

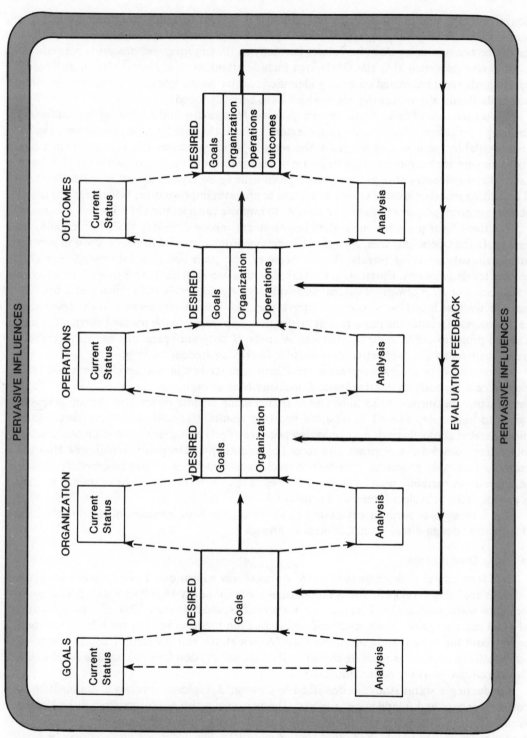

Figure 1. Schematic for the improvement design

effectively identify and improve curriculum goals, it is helpful to understand the philosophy or assumptions underlying the program. If current goals and philosophy appear to be incompatible, steps can be taken to bring them into closer harmony as the improvement process is carried out.

It is also important that the Goals area include attention to students' educational needs. Program goals should be based on clearly identified learner needs. Priorities for acting on established goals should also reflect the needs which have been identified.

The second area of focus, Organization, provides for a review and analysis of several factors influencing curriculum effectiveness. These factors include: the specific programs offered, the resources available and how they are used, the ways in which processes like communication and decision making are handled, and the structure or arrangement of the school or district. Although organizational influences have generally been given little or no explicit attention in development and evaluation models, this area is very important to program improvement. When organizational problems are given proper attention it is possible to improve the operation of all school programs.

The third focal point for curriculum improvement involves the day to day functioning of programs. In the Operations area, curriculum implementation is studied to assess how well general educational goals are being translated into course or unit goals and then into specific learning objectives for daily lessons. Curriculum workers should take a systematic look at ways to improve the sequencing or arrangement of content and skills across grade levels and subject areas. Instructional effectiveness is also an important concern that has a direct relationship to the operations area. Instruction includes the important activities that help translate the planned curriculum into the actual program experienced by students. A study of program operations can help teachers increase their repertoire of effective strategies for improving student learning.

Outcomes of the program represent the fourth area studied in this development and evaluation process. In early evaluation models, measurement of outcomes was the important focal point. Outcome measurement should be viewed from a much broader perspective. Attention should be given to unintended as well as intended program results. Curricula which are successfully achieving stated academic goals may be having negative effects on student motivation or attitudes. In other cases, benefits of a program may exceed gains anticipated by program planners. How the outcomes affect other programs, or influence teachers and students, should be carefully considered. Procedures currently used to assess outcomes of the program need to be examined so they can provide valid, reliable information for future decision making.

The four areas of focus briefly described above are the basic elements of the development and evaluation design discussed in Chapters 4 through 7.

The Status Descriptions

It is very helpful to describe the current status of any educational program when improvement plans are being developed. Status descriptions are preliminary overviews which include some information about program goals, organization, operations, and outcomes. This information, gathered at an early stage of the development and evaluation process, helps to provide a clear perspective about the current state of the program. Although the status descriptions are portrayed schematically in Figure 1 as separate elements, they are usually developed during the set of initial activities referred to as the status study.

Conducting a status study, as described in Chapter 3, typically involves a combination of document analyses and interviews or surveys. The pertinent written information will be located in such documents as: curriculum guides, accreditation reports, Board of Education minutes, faculty handbooks, course syllabi, and other similar materials. The document analysis may be brief or fairly extensive. Similarly, the use of interviews or surveys can be expected to vary according to the local situation. It is advisable to obtain at least some information from representative teachers, administrators, other staff members, parents, and students. This wide range of viewpoints is most helpful in identifying important differences of opinion as well as commonly held perceptions about the current curriculum.

Status portrayal should be a reasonably short and straightforward activity with the expectation that additional descriptive information will be generated in later phases of the improvement process. Data obtained during the status study are likely to suggest possible recommendations for improving the program. This information must not be acted on until analysis activities are completed.

The status study generally has its major impact on the improvement design itself. Designs or plans of action which are in harmony with current local conditions have a much greater chance of success. Curriculum workers can identify through the status study those areas they need to focus on in depth and those that require less attention. Thus, status descriptions often lead to more efficient use of the resources available for curriculum improvement.

The Analysis Activities

Once a determination of current status has been made, activities designed to analyze the worth and effectiveness of the present program can begin. In the designated "analysis" components, the types of activities most commonly associated with evaluation are conducted. Curriculum goals, organization, operations, and outcomes are screened and assessed to see what steps might be needed to improve the educational program.

When conducting the program analysis, those responsible for curriculum improvement are able to use status study information and gather additional data as needed. A variety of data collection strategies can be used to conduct the curriculum analysis. Observations, interviews, questionnaires, tests, attitude scales, and indirect indicators are among the most common ways of gathering needed information. Key questions posed in advance can help determine what information is required and how to obtain it. Very often, asking the right questions is one of the most important factors in carrying out an effective program improvement process. With practice, curriculum workers can become much more skillful in asking questions that will generate facts and insights needed to strengthen all phases of the educational program.

As analysis activities proceed, decisions are regularly called for about discrepancies or mismatches that may exist between current and expected program functions. Appropriate criteria or standards must be considered in these decision making activities. These may be derived from professional association guidelines, research reports, needs assessments, or other sources. The analysis process is best viewed as a dynamic set of activities designed to sift, assess, and make judgments about the information made available through various data sources. When done well, it leads to recommendations for improvement that will have a positive impact on the local situation and the students being served.

The Curriculum Improvement Components

As the development and evaluation process is carried out, a pattern of crosschecking and refining emerges. Status study information is regularly reviewed in conducting the analysis activities. At the same time, insights gained while answering the analysis questions help develop a clearer understanding of the current program. The interplay of status and analysis activities makes it possible to recommend needed adjustments involving any of the four major areas being examined. Due to the ongoing, systematic nature of the process, there is no need to wait for all areas to be analyzed before action can be taken to improve the program.

In the schematic framework, four Cumulative Improvement Components are used to represent the gradual development of a set of recommendations and action plans. Following each major area of analysis, a clearer picture of the desired curriculum is obtained. Goal analysis activities, for example, may lead to the agreement that present goals are appropriate, or may result in the adoption of a revised set of goals. The first component depicts the improvement of the Goals area based on status and analysis activities.

During the Organization phase, knowledge of the desired goals provides an updated referent point. Status descriptions of program organization can be interpreted and assessed in light of newly developed goals as well as prior expectations. While selected organizational analysis activities may be initiated before desired goals are finalized and adopted, this phase would not be considered complete until agreed upon goals and desired organizational features are in harmony. The second cumulative improvement component depicts the next step in the refinement process.

It is important to note that the desired curriculum may involve little or no change from the current program. The value of a systematic process lies not in the extent of the changes made, but in the fact that all major areas are analyzed separately and then together to be sure the program is as effective as possible. When major changes are required or new programs developed, the cumulative approach distributes needed changes across time and helps ensure that each important change has the best chance for lasting success.

The cumulative improvement components following the Operations and Outcomes areas in the framework reflect a gradual, success oriented change strategy. In each phase of development and evaluation, the results of prior analyses are incorporated and extended, with ample opportunity to make additional corrections as needed.

The Pervasive Influences

Surrounding the schematic in Figure 1 a band is used to portray the diverse influences that affect curriculum improvement efforts. These influences include: social and political forces; special interest groups; local, state, or national legislation or policies; funding patterns; large scale testing programs; and commercial textbook publishers. It is important that those engaged in curriculum development and evaluation look beyond the immediate situation to consider how their work is being affected by external factors. Sometimes these effects are direct and easy to identify. Even then it may be difficult to provide an appropriate response. In other cases, subtle but pervasive influences such as gradual demographic changes affect the educational program. Discovering the roles of both types of major influences can be accomplished with a comprehensive improvement design. A careful portrayal of current status can be especially helpful in understanding pervasive influences in the local setting.

A Comprehensive Look at Educational Improvement

Program improvement takes place in the broad context of a total system of education. There are several subsystems which are clearly interrelated. The framework presented in Figure 2 illustrates how development and evaluation processes relate to personal evaluation and staff development. When considered as a total system, these three interacting subsystems help establish the conditions needed to achieve agreed upon educational goals.

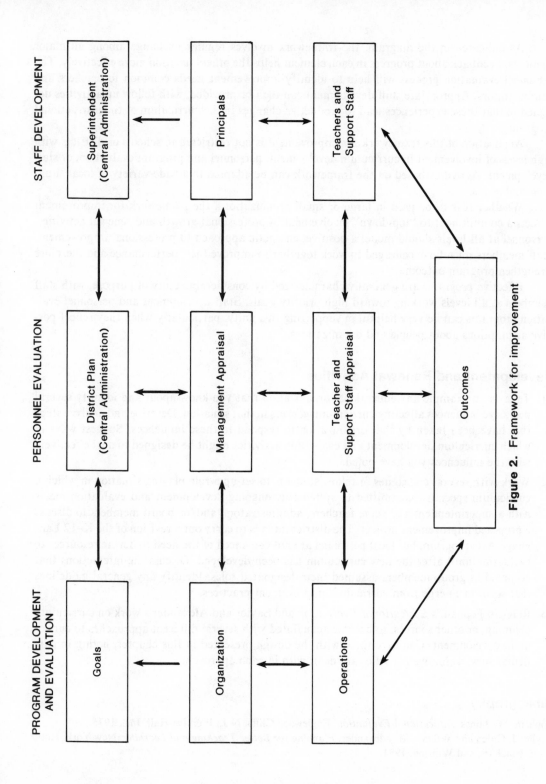

Figure 2. Framework for improvement

STAFF DEVELOPMENT

- Superintendent (Central Administration)
- Principals
- Teachers and Support Staff

PERSONNEL EVALUATION

- District Plan (Central Administration)
- Management Appraisal
- Teacher and Support Staff Appraisal
- Outcomes

PROGRAM DEVELOPMENT AND EVALUATION

- Goals
- Organization
- Operations

As indicated in the diagram, the framework involves regular exchange among all major elements. Feedback about progress in each element helps the others function more effectively. The personnel evaluation process will help to identify improvement needs common to teachers and administrators. Appropriate staff development can then be provided, with follow up activities designed so that these experiences lead to productive changes in the curriculum or the instructional program.

Application of this framework for improvement is not restricted to schools or districts with high levels of involvement in curriculum development, personnel and program evaluation, or staff development. Activities based on the framework can be adapted to a wide variety of local situations and needs.

Whether it is to be used in large or small organizations, the framework for improvement reflects a commitment to "top-down" involvement in professional growth and renewal activities. Personnel at all levels should model a positive, energetic approach to professional improvement. Staff members must be encouraged to work together to improve their performance and therefore strengthen program outcomes.

Effective programs are generally characterized by considerable unity of purpose, with staff members at all levels working toward high priority goals. Staff development and personnel evaluation programs can be very helpful in supporting this unity, particularly when they reflect positive assumptions about people and organizations.

Development and Renewal Activities

1. Take as an example any educational organization that you know about and identify several pervasive influences affecting curriculum workers in that situation. Describe and analyze steps that have been taken by that organization to respond to these influences. Suggest ways in which curriculum development and evaluation activities might be designed to deal effectively with the influences you have noted.

2. Work with several colleagues or fellow students to set up a role playing situation in which a curriculum specialist committed to systematic, ongoing development and evaluation meets with a superintendent and some teachers, administrators, and/or board members to discuss a proposed improvement project. The district intends to carry out a revision of the K–12 Language Arts program, but local personnel are not convinced of the need to devote resources to evaluation until after the new curriculum has been developed. Discuss the interactions that occurred as group members assumed their designated roles. Identify any general guidelines that seem to emerge from curriculum improvement practices.

3. Refer to Popham's *Educational Evaluation* and Saylor and Alexander's work on curriculum planning, or other sources, to become acquainted with several different approaches to curriculum development. Compare these with the design presented in this chapter, noting in particular how evaluative activities are dealt with in each approach.

Bibliography

Popham, W. James. *Educational Evaluation.* Englewood Cliffs, N.J.: Prentice-Hall, Inc., 1975.

Saylor, J. Galen and William M. Alexander. *Planning for Better Teaching and Learning.* New York: Holt, Rinehart, and Winston, 1981.

Chapter 3

Initiating the Development and Evaluation Process: Determining Current Status

Introduction

It is generally agreed that curriculum improvement activities are most effective when attention is paid to the various factors influencing the local school or district. These pervasive influences vary considerably in the degree and subtlety of their impact on curriculum workers. Some can be classified on the basis of jurisdictional level such as local, state, regional, and national. Others may be viewed in terms of legal implications resulting from court decisions and legislation.

This chapter focuses on several important factors which influence curriculum development and evaluation activities in local schools and districts. Attention is given to how these factors affect decision making at different stages of the development and evaluation process. By examining the types of influences operating in the local setting, a basis is established for successfully initiating and sustaining program improvement activities. The ideas presented in this chapter for generating descriptions of current status provide a practical starting point for curriculum improvement efforts.

Becoming Aware of Pervasive Influences

The events reviewed in Chapter 1 highlighted the pervasive influence of standardized testing programs on curriculum development and evaluation. This concern for measurement of educational outcomes has persisted to the present day, and has been extended in many states by recent legislation mandating competency or proficiency testing.

The important influence of textbooks and materials was also evident in reviewing the background of curriculum development and evaluation. Very often the adopted textbooks have been the major determinant of the school curriculum, affecting both the nature of and sequence of ideas encountered by students. Since most of these texts and associated materials have been developed for regional or national audiences, curriculum workers must be especially careful to examine these resources in relation to local needs, goals, and programs. As more emphasis is placed on self contained learning packages and multi-year skill development materials, decision makers have an even greater obligation to acquire and utilize the best possible evaluation information when developing local programs.

Numerous examples could be cited to indicate the ways that federal financing and influence have led to changes in local program development. One of the earliest instances of large scale federal involvement was the Smith-Hughes Act of 1917. This legislation resulted in the development of agricultural, industrial, and home economics programs across the country. Smith-Hughes programs enjoyed a high degree of autonomy from local influence. Although the programs were generally successful, many educators questioned the high degree of external regulation of locally based programs.

Since the early to middle 1960's massive federal funding has been provided for diverse educational programs. The Elementary and Secondary Education Acts of 1965 and the Vocational Education Acts of the same period responded to contemporary social influences. A variety of compensatory education programs and early childhood education programs resulted from those influences. Subsequently, career education, education of students with special needs, and multicultural education emerged as federal funding priorities.

Many states have developed programs that have expanded the financing available for these new curricula. When such extensive funding is available to the schools, programs are often developed and implemented whether or not they fit the needs of local clients. It is important for those associated with education to understand the implications of this add on approach to program development. The phenomenon has often resulted in a situation termed the "patchwork curriculum."

Given recent declines in educational funding levels, curriculum workers must be particularly alert to another potential problem, inappropriate cutbacks in programs and services. When budgets are threatened, it has been common for decision makers to sharply reduce or eliminate fine arts, vocational courses, physical education, and other programs which may be regarded by certain segments of the public as "frills." Economic conditions clearly represent important pervasive influences which must be considered whenever curriculum improvement efforts are initiated.

In a growing number of states, legislators have been enacting statutes with major curriculum implications. Requirements concerning minimum expectations for graduation, generally accompanied by proficiency testing programs, essentially mandate that certain goals be met at the local level. State boards of education have played a similar role in establishing statewide goals for education. It is important for those concerned with curriculum improvement to recognize the extent to which such practices imply the loss of local control over important educational decisions. State or federal curriculum decision making is inconsistent with the concept of local control of education. The needs and values of local citizens and educators may be in conflict with these mandates.

There are clearly a number of other factors which can be identified as major curriculum influences. Various special interest groups have begun to affect curriculum decisions. There are groups that screen reading material while others are trying to control the teaching of evolution and other controversial topics. Also, political influences on education have been evident, resulting in part from the structure of school systems and the processes for selecting school officials. Accreditation activities have affected the types of programs offered and the allocation of resources in the local school setting.

In order to successfully deal with the various influences on educational programs, a systematic process is needed for strengthening development and evaluation at the local level. The first step in the process is to conduct a status study of the existing educational program.

Status Description: Goals

Sound development and evaluation processes depend on accurate information about the present state of affairs in the local setting. Failure to develop a clear picture of existing conditions, including the perceptions of those currently affected by the educational system, seriously hinders development and evaluation efforts.

A study of the present status is to a large extent an information gathering effort. Data acquired during the status study are utilized at various stages of the development and evaluation process. It is therefore especially important to gather appropriate types and amounts of information about the local context. However, care should be taken to gather only information essential to the development of the status study. Generating unnecessary information creates data management problems as well as alienating those involved with the study.

The goals area is generally the first to receive attention in preparing the status descriptions. Although written documents may be found which contain philosophy statements and educational goals, such materials are often incomplete or outdated. In other cases there may be no written philosophy or goal statements available. If satisfactory documents cannot be obtained, steps can be taken during the status study to generate information about unstated goals.

Before considering these steps, it may be well to clarify the purpose for examining philosophy and goals. The philosophy statement useful in curriculum development and evaluation is one which clearly and simply sets forth major assumptions regarding the process of education. Philosophy statements may include: preferred student and teacher roles, the emphasis placed on various skill or knowledge areas, and the beliefs held regarding values and moral development. Goals are closely related to these philosophical assumptions, stating in declarative form the expected outcomes of educational programs. Awareness of the school or district's beliefs and educational goals is necessary if curriculum workers are to be effective in program planning and improvement.

Assumptions and goals may be determined in a status study by conducting interviews with selected teachers, administrators, community members, and students. If major differences in perception are identified as a result of these interviews, appropriate activities similar to those described in Chapter 4 can be carried out to help the district reach agreement on philosophy and goal statements.

Another procedure for generating information is to conduct an analysis of all relevant documents. This content analysis would be applied to school board minutes, policy manuals and administrative handbooks, curriculum guides and materials in use, and recent accreditation reports.

It is also important for curriculum developers and evaluators to be aware of the relative emphasis currently placed on different types of goals. Although priorities may not be stated in writing, they can be inferred by studying how resources are allocated. The utilization of time, money, facilities, personnel, and other resources provides a valuable indicator of local priorities. The status study will help to determine if local priorities are consistent with the stated goals.

For example, in one school district, resources for art and music programs had been severely curtailed, although the clients of the schools voiced strong support for aesthetic education as a curriculum goal. This type of information can help the curriculum developer and evaluator plan the activities needed to establish appropriate local goals and priorities.

Several other factors related to philosophy and goals are pertinent in conducting the status study. It is important to examine the compatibility of existing goals with local beliefs and values. How students, parents, and educators perceive the relative worth of current goals affects their acceptance and may determine the level of support given school system programs.

Another factor to consider when studying current status is the process used to develop the existing philosophy and goals. Information about who was involved and what types of activities took place can be very helpful. It enables curriculum workers to understand if current documents were developed with the involvement of a wide range of personnel or by a minimum of client input.

Status Description: Organization

While local philosophy, goals, and priorities are being examined during the status study, it is also possible to generate some useful information about resources, roles, responsibilities, and current programs. The importance of these factors makes it advisable to take a systematic look at the current functioning of the educational organization.

Organizational considerations are generally underrated as significant influences on the attainment of educational goals. Clearly delineated goals and agreed upon priorities cannot in themselves counteract ineffective organizational procedures. However, a smoothly functioning organization can provide substantial support to the educational programs being offered.

In preparing a status description of the organization, an initial area of interest may be current patterns of authority and responsibility in relation to curricular and instructional decision making. While studying one school district it was found that no one would claim responsibility for making curriculum decisions. This lack of clarity about responsibilities made the curriculum development and evaluation process generally ineffectual. Poorly defined or misunderstood roles and responsibilities can cause problems to be left unsolved. Opportunities for positive action are likely to be missed and conflicts among staff members may be created.

Questions regarding role, responsibility, and authority can generally be answered through a series of interviews or discussions with selected personnel. Written position descriptions may also be available for review and analysis.

The same techniques can also be used to review existing communication patterns. The effects of poor communication on all types of curriculum activities can be serious and long lasting. A breakdown in communication prevents the flow of accurate, timely information needed to maintain positive and productive working relationships.

In the study of current status, typical communication patterns are identified. Some organizations utilize a vertical communication process with most messages either filtering down through the system or up to higher organizational levels. In other organizations, communication may be primarily vertical but does not include two way transmission of messages. For the communication process to be most effective, two way vertical communication should go hand in hand with the horizontal flow of information. Horizontal communication encourages the exchange of ideas among peers and helps generate a greater sense of shared purpose.

A preliminary look at current program offerings and how various programs are organized is another useful part of the status study. The purpose of this brief portrayal is to better understand what programs presently exist, how they were developed, and how they are organized within the overall school or district curriculum. Reviewing the arrangement of programs being offered generates information needed to plan future development and evaluation activities. Information from the status study can help to determine the "fit" among identified goals and priorities, the effect of previous efforts of curriculum committees or other groups, and the programs currently available to the students.

As part of the organizational status description, all special projects need to be identified. Many schools and districts have numerous small projects in operation which do not have an apparent relationship to overall curriculum planning. In a medium sized district recently studied, more than eighty such special projects were found. A large number of these bore little if any relationship to the goals and priorities that had been formally established by that school system.

Resource allocation for special programs as well as for components of the established curriculum should also be examined during the status study. The assignment of teachers to schools and subject areas, the allocation of support personnel, and other patterns of human resource utilization are especially helpful in depicting local priorities.

It is important to include a description of current curriculum development and evaluation activities in the status study. Information about these activities can help clarify what is being done to determine and carry out needed curriculum improvements. Identifying those who have responsibility for curriculum development and evaluation is a particularly important part of this portrayal. By noting any current planning efforts, recommendations which result from the status study can be used to suggest procedures which will be in harmony with long range improvement plans.

Status Description: Operations

To accurately portray the current curriculum, a status study should include descriptions of day to day activities and events associated with curriculum implementation. Observation of a sample of classes representing various grade levels and subject areas can provide an excellent overview about how current programs are functioning.

The status description of operational factors helps curriculum developers and evaluators understand how well the current philosophy, goals and priorities are translated into action on a day to day basis. For example, science goals may be regarded in a given district as very important learning outcomes. However, observers may find that little emphasis is actually being placed on science instruction while reading and mathematics receive most of the attention in the primary and elementary grades.

Agreed upon local goals and priorities should be evident in objective written descriptions of classroom events. Allocation of instructional time is one useful indicator of the relative priority being given to various goals and objectives within the curriculum. Information about clubs, sports, field trips, guidance opportunities, and other non-classroom experiences within the curriculum also indicates the agreement between stated beliefs and actual expectations.

Another focal point in the operations status study is the process used to monitor curriculum implementation. Monitoring helps ensure that teachers are following the agreed upon curriculum in day to day instruction. It is helpful in this context to identify current supervision practices. Interviews with selected teachers and administrators can indicate the nature and frequency of classroom visitations. They can also help clarify how information and recommendations emerging from the current supervision process are used for evaluation and instructional improvement. Bellon and Bellon (1982) have developed a supervision program that has been found to be effective in monitoring the curriculum and improving instruction.

In many cases, failure to establish a systematic process for improving instruction results in a lack of awareness about how effectively the planned curriculum is being put into action. A better understanding of these important operational factors acquired during the status study can lead to successful improvement in later phases of the curriculum development and evaluation process.

Improvement of program operations can be greatly facilitated by an effective staff development program. As areas of shared concern are identified and specific staff development needs recognized, it is important to provide experiences that will encourage professional growth of the staff. Therefore, the status study should be designed to examine the types of staff development activities that have been provided or are currently available.

It is also useful to obtain information about the involvement of various individuals and groups in planning, conducting, or participating in staff development activities. Staff development has all too often been viewed as a process applicable only to teachers, with administrators involved primarily in planning or scheduling activities. The importance and complexity of the responsibilities exercised by personnel at all levels of the organization has made this one sided approach obsolete. Administrators should be involved in regular improvement activities relevant to their professional roles. Conducting a status study which examines the current approach to staff development provides information for future decision making about development and renewal programs.

Status Description: Outcomes

Although the detailed analysis of educational outcomes occurs at a later stage of the development and evaluation process, the status study should include an initial look at outcomes of the curriculum. Local documents can provide useful information about how well students have generally performed on standardized tests of academic achievement. Other types of measurement data, including grade reports and results of specialized testing programs, may also be reviewed as part of this status description.

A preliminary analysis of educational outcomes can be important in identifying the procedures used locally to determine how well educational goals are being attained. Strategies for assessing goal attainment in the local setting should reflect established priorities. They should include clearly defined procedures for providing feedback for improvement. Further, attention should be given on a regular basis to the possible side effects or unintended outcomes of programs being offered, such as changes in attitudes or career interests. Determining the nature of current practices in this area can generally be accomplished through interviews of selected individuals in the local school or system. The information acquired can be especially useful in subsequently analyzing and revising goals, organization, and operations to improve learning opportunities.

Relationship to Other Development and Evaluation Approaches

A comprehensive status study can contribute significantly to the portrayal of four major areas: goals, organization, operations, and outcomes. These areas are treated in greater depth in Chapters 4 through 7, with detailed explanations about how information acquired during the status study provides a basis for successful curriculum improvement.

Recommending that a status study be conducted to initiate curriculum improvement efforts is highly compatible with the belief that development and evaluation are complementary, interacting processes. Evaluation is viewed in the status study and the activities which follow as a supportive process that is inseparable from curriculum development.

The status study approach described in this chapter is related to several well known evaluation models and processes. The concept of context evaluation, involving a full description of the setting in which evaluation is to take place, is part of the decision oriented CIPP model developed by Stufflebeam. Antecedent evaluation has a similar function in Stake's judgmental evaluation model, which establishes the degree of congruence between intended and observed events. In antecedent evaluation, a careful exploration of the factors which have preceded and led to current practices are examined.

Other examples could be cited to show the general agreement that exists concerning the need to establish a context or perspective for development and evaluation efforts. The approach that has been presented in this chapter goes beyond most current frameworks by providing specific guidelines to help curriculum workers achieve success in these activities. The time needed to describe present status is well worth investing in order to develop a solid base for educational improvement in the local setting.

Development and Renewal Activities

1. Identify a specific educational program with which you are familiar. You may choose a course or an academic area within the program or a specific project related to one area of the curriculum. If you prefer, you may focus instead on a broader program, such as the total elementary curriculum of a particular school or district. Develop a brief description of the goals, organization, operations, and outcomes of this program, referring to the guidelines presented in the chapter. For this "mini" status study, rely as much as needed on your own perceptions and on existing information accessible to you. Discuss the program with others, if possible, to help increase the accuracy of your portrayal.

2. The status study provides early opportunities for participation by local personnel and clients. Analyze at least one curriculum improvement project or activity which you have seen implemented or know about. Explain how a status study might have helped to strengthen the project and reduce obstacles to successful implementation.

3. Discuss with peers or colleagues the ways in which the pervasive influences affecting programs with which you are most familiar have shifted through the years. Develop a list of key questions that can be asked in a status study to gather accurate, up to date information about major influences on the curriculum.

Bibliography

Popham, W. James. *Educational Evaluation.* Englewood Cliffs, N.J.: Prentice-Hall, Inc., 1975.

Saylor, J. Galen and William M. Alexander. *Planning for Better Teaching and Learning.* New York: Holt, Rinehart, and Winston, 1981.

Worthen, Blaine R. and James K. Sanders. *Educational Evaluation: Theory and Practice.* Worthington, Ohio: Charles A. Jones Publishing Co., 1973.

Annotated Bibliography

Bellon, J. J. and E. C. Bellon. *Classroom Supervision and Instructional Improvement,* 2nd Edition. Dubuque: Kendall/Hunt Publishing Co., 1982. The authors describe a supervisory process for improved instruction. The topics of leadership, renewal, and evaluation are developed around a cooperative process which includes a pre observation conference, data based observation, and a post observation conference.

McGregor, Douglas. *The Human Side of Enterprise.* New York: McGraw-Hill Book Co., 1960. The author presents the theory that the assumptions leaders hold about people determine the whole character of the enterprise. These are known as Theory X and Theory Y assumptions.

Chapter 4

Establishing Goals and Priorities

Introduction

In Chapter 3, a process for acquiring preliminary information about the current curriculum was described. One of the major activities of that process was to describe the status of existing goals and priorities. Suggested focal points included previous goal setting activities, how they were conducted, and who was involved.

It is important to the development and evaluation process to take whatever steps are needed to establish an agreed upon set of educational goals for the curriculum. While there are several characteristics to look for in an effective goal setting process, decisions must be made to select techniques appropriate to each specific situation.

The status description of current goals is especially useful in making goal setting decisions. If the district has recently adopted a set of educational goals and has not undergone any major population changes, a decision may be made to focus on simple follow up activities. These would be designed to verify local acceptance and understanding of the goals. On the other hand, districts lacking agreed upon goals or exhibiting confusion over priorities should engage in more extensive goal setting activities.

In the sections that follow, several strategies are presented which can be used to establish educational goals. Basic definitions and assumptions that can guide the goal setting activities are discussed. Since the goal setting phase of development and evaluation serves as a cornerstone to the entire process, it is especially important to understand the implications of the various goal setting approaches. Several propositions are presented that describe conditions necessary for successful goal setting programs.

Basic Concepts and Definitions

Since the early 1900's there have been a number of commissions and other professional groups that have proposed general goals for education or for specific areas such as secondary education. In addition, state and local goal setting activities have resulted in numerous sets of expectations intended to guide educational programs. A growing interest in the goals and purposes of public education has arisen in part from external pressure for accountability. Concern for curriculum reorganization and reform has also been a factor in generating increased attention to goal setting activities.

Despite the recent emphasis on educational goals, many educators remain skeptical about their value. Such feelings tend to dissipate when a clearer understanding is gained about the specific roles that properly developed goal statements can play in efforts to improve student learning.

Educational goals are defined as timeless and nonmeasurable statements of desired outcomes. Goal statements should reflect the values of those involved in, or directly affected by, the educational program. It is important for each program to have an identified purpose or direction that can be easily understood and communicated to all interested participants. Clear goal statements should help establish this desired sense of purpose and direction.

The term, educational needs, is often used in discussions of goals and goal setting processes. Although it is not uncommon to hear the terms used virtually as synonyms, needs and goals have different definitions and serve different functions in development and evaluation. Educational needs are most appropriately viewed as an important data source for establishing goals.

Information about needs reveals where gaps or discrepancies exist between current program outcomes and desired outcomes. One may think of educational needs as differences between how students are presently performing in a certain area and the expectations held about their performance.

When differences are found between current and desired performance, several possibilities exist. If students are currently falling short of expected performance in a particular area, an unmet need may be indicated. Major unmet needs may become the basis for assigning priorities to particular goals. These goal statements then give impetus and direction to program planning, resource allocation, and other activities which should assist in meeting the identified needs.

It is also possible that a comparison of current and expected performance may reveal areas where present performance exceeds expectations. Discrepancies of this type may be thought of as met needs and may indicate programs which have received resources and attention beyond their perceived importance or value. Met needs may also be found in situations where programs were established to fulfill needs that for one reason or another no longer exist. While such situations may be indicative of past success, it is crucial that goals for the future be written to direct resources to major unmet needs. Goals reflecting met needs as well as areas where performance and expectations are closely matched should not generally be given highest priority in short term program planning.

However, there are important programs that previously have been assigned a high priority, have achieved their goals, and should be continued as high priority programs. The priority assigned to any goals or programs should be determined by ongoing student needs. Goals developed from or consistent with student needs should give direction to the total educational program.

Educational goals, then, are statements of expectations which give direction, are timeless, and are future oriented. They help organizations develop plans for meeting current and future needs. By serving as an important referent point for program development and evaluation, goals become essential to local educational improvement efforts.

Propositions about Goals

Before discussing procedures for establishing and assessing goals, several points to provide a frame of reference are presented. The propositions discussed below have been influenced by philosophical assumptions, theoretical principles, and guidelines developed from improvement projects conducted in a variety of educational settings.

It appears essential that those giving leadership to program improvement examine propositions such as these to help clarify their views about goal setting. This analysis can help ensure that plans for improving curriculum are compatible with local beliefs and at the same time consistent with sound theory and practice. The following statements are proposed for consideration.

A. **Goal statements should represent the values of all appropriate client groups.** When goals are established, every attempt should be made to involve participants who represent all population subgroups in the community: students, teachers and administrators, other professional educators, parents, and adults who do not have children in the schools. This does not mean that each group should develop a set of goals but that their expectations, values, and aspirations are considered when goals are established.

In some situations, there may be close agreement concerning the appropriate role of the school and the types of learning outcomes perceived as most worthwhile. When the different groups served by the educational system share common values regarding education, curriculum workers can generally count on a strong support base as they move toward fulfilling these mutually held expectations.

However, it is more typical for differences to exist among the various groups concerned with educational outcomes. Students may value career preparation and training for their future personal and professional roles, while their parents and teachers place more emphasis on preparation for further academic study. In some communities there are important differences between those who value a traditional program emphasizing basic skills and those who strongly favor a more diversified curriculum.

It is necessary to identify different value positions and deal openly with them in the goal setting process. When the deeply rooted beliefs of one or more major client groups are left hidden, it is not possible to develop plans that will prevent them from causing serious alienation. There can be no guarantee, of course, that all major differences will ever be resolved or all groups fully satisfied. However, productive discussion and an exchange of ideas can be initiated by the goal setting process. Activities can be planned to bring members of various groups together to talk about education in a positive context.

When results of these activities are publicized in the community, local beliefs and aspirations can be understood and appreciated by a larger segment of the population. Making an honest effort to involve a wide range of participants in setting educational goals creates positive attitudes about the process. These in turn tend to generate greater support for the educational program. The participants do not need to be involved in making decisions about the final goals, but they must know that their values have been carefully considered. The long term effect is to develop increased public support for improving the educational program.

B. **The process of generating and agreeing upon educational goals should be designed to help schools become renewing and future oriented organizations.** When people are asked to state their expectations and aspirations for education, they tend to identify future needs or wants. Values are implied in statements about what students should be able to do when they finish their schooling. This process results in looking toward the future, even though the stated expectations may be based on past experiences.

The extent to which educational programs can become backward looking rather than future oriented may not be recognized. Tradition and precedents that have been established may be cited as justification for maintaining current practice. Programs that failed in the past can serve as an excuse for not attempting to improve current programs. Whether conscious or unconscious in origin, the overemphasis on the past has been found to be detrimental to positive growth and renewal. It is important to understand how to promote a healthy balance between past practice and future development and evaluation activities.

An effective goal setting process can serve as one such strategy. As students, parents, teachers, and others consider their goals and expectations, they can be encouraged to focus on the programs that can exist as well as those currently available. It is a well known principle of motivation that having a clear sense of purpose stimulates people to greater effort and enthusiasm. When opportunities are provided for an active role in setting educational goals, these powerful sources of motivation can more readily be tapped. The positive effects of forward looking behavior in educational organizations clearly indicate that the time and energy needed to reach agreement on desired goals are very worthwhile ingredients in improvement programs.

C. **Priority levels of educational goals should be used as a basis for decision making.** A well designed goal setting process should generate information useful in determining which goals have higher priority in the local setting. For example, goals which reflect major unmet needs merit higher priority than those which are based on small discrepancies between current performance and expectations. In addition, goals which are strongly supported by such concerned groups as students and teachers will generally be assigned higher priority than those favored by just a few. The development and evaluation process should include activities leading to agreement on the goals to be accorded high priority in the local school system.

Agreement on a limited number of top priority goals is an important step toward sound planning and decision making. This is particularly true in situations where limited resources, including human as well as material support, must be dispersed to fulfill a large number of obligations and provide a wide range of services. Declining student populations, along with increased costs and reduced funding bases, have made judicious resource allocation imperative.

Priorities need to be established to assist those who must make crucial decisions concerning resources, program changes, and other related matters. Without clear priorities, decision makers can find themselves working at cross purposes, to the detriment of all concerned. Political forces operating in these situations can also threaten to become too influential when accepted goals and priorities are not consulted as referent points for decision making.

As conditions change and different needs emerge, priorities among goals should be expected to change. Success in meeting particular learner needs may result in lower priority for the related goal statements when future plans are developed. Such goals might take on "maintenance" status, with some additional resources becoming available to serve other needs that remain unmet or that have been recently identified. Decision making should be based on timely feedback about the program and its effects on students being served. In order to obtain the best possible feedback, current goals and priorities should be made known to all concerned with the program.

D. **Educational goals should be written, made public, and evaluated on a regular basis.** Educators sometimes say they have goals, but refuse to put them in writing or make them public. If goals are not in writing it becomes very difficult to discuss them or to analyze them for meaning or appropriateness. Once the statements are in writing they can be carefully examined and when necessary adjusted or refined.

Educational goals should be made public so that all interested persons are reminded about the goals of the schools. Posting goal statements in school buildings and publishing them in handbooks, curriculum guides, and newsletters can help maintain attention on the achievement of these important outcomes. Well publicized goals cause informal evaluation to occur on a regular basis. Formal evaluation of the goals should also be carried out regularly and systematically based on changing population patterns, environmental influences, and student needs.

Although the goal statements are timeless and do not specify target dates for attainment, they need to be reviewed regularly to determine if they are giving direction to current expectations. An evaluation of the existing or proposed goals, guided by key questions to help assess their appropriateness and worth, is an important component of a systematic development and evaluation process. Strategies for setting and analyzing educational goals are described in the remainder of this chapter. As noted previously, the plan of action adopted in a specific situation needs to build on up to date information about current program status and local conditions.

Alternatives for Setting Educational Goals

When status description and analysis activities reveal inadequacies in present educational goals, plans need to be developed for generating statements which reflect desired outcomes of the program. In the following sections, three types of goal setting approaches are briefly described to provide an indication of the range of current practice. They are set in the context of systemwide goal setting, but all may be applied to a more limited context such as specific programs, projects, or courses.

As the three major approaches or their variations are considered for adaptation and use in the local setting, it may be helpful to think about several general questions. Curriculum workers who are about to design a plan of action for establishing goals may wish to consider:

1. How much community involvement does this process generate?
2. What is the anticipated level of involvement of administrators, teachers, other system personnel, and students?
3. To what extent is the process based on local philosophy and educational beliefs?
4. How actively are local staff to be involved in developing procedures to be used to gather and analyze data?
5. How much time should be allowed to carry out this process effectively?

Answers to these questions can be compared with local intents, resources, and constraints in order to make decisions about the desired course of action. The importance of solid goal setting practices cannot be overstated. The goal statements that are derived serve an important role in planning programs, allocating resources, and assessing curriculum effectiveness.

Before presenting the three alternative approaches to be discussed, a brief overview of past and present practice in this area may be helpful. One of the earliest and most enduring approaches to establishing educational outcomes was through commissions or other special groups.

The practice of using committees or commissions to deal with educational goal setting had its beginning near the turn of the century. Several such groups were established to study and set goals for education. Their efforts generated considerable attention at the time. Even today, the work of the Committee of Ten (1893) and particularly the Commission on the Reorganization of Secondary Education (1918) with its well known "Cardinal Principles" continues to stimulate discussion and influence current thinking about educational goals. Since that early period, numerous groups have been constituted at the national, regional, state, and local levels to engage in goal setting activities.

The commission or committee approach clearly limits the amount of direct participation by persons within or served by the educational system. However, groups of this type, often referred to as task forces, are still widely used. Statewide curricula in such current interest areas as family living, nutrition education, or career education may have goals developed through committee deliberation.

Members of task forces, generally representing a variety of academic and professional specializations, can use a number of different data sources to help them establish program goals. It is possible, for instance, to apply Tyler's framework for rational curriculum planning to guide committee efforts. When using this framework, information about the students, society, and subject matter is compiled as a basis for tentative goal setting. Philosophical beliefs and psychological principles serve as screens to help the group filter out inappropriate or unworthy goal statements. Agreed upon goals are subsequently refined into more specific objectives as the planning process continues.

Current approaches to goal setting are likely to be designed to secure more active and widespread participation by local constituents. Small group meetings may be held to determine participants' reactions to lists of prepared goal statements or to open ended questions about their expectations and perceptions regarding school programs.

Survey techniques have also gained increased popularity in goal setting processes, enabling a wide audience to be involved. If steps are taken to help ensure an adequate and representative set of responses, the use of questionnaires can be a valuable tool in the goal setting process.

The most important consideration is not the data gathering technique itself but the spirit and intent of the goal setting effort. The approach selected should be consistent with beliefs held about the value of educational goals and their role in the overall development and evaluation process.

The Clean Slate Process

As the name implies, the clean slate approach to educational goal setting begins with no predetermined outcomes set forth. The first step in this process, which has also been called the blank sheet approach, involves collecting information from the various local population groups about what they feel the schools should be achieving. This general information can come from discussions, interviews, or meetings, with the results used by advisory groups or other designated teams to develop a preliminary list of tentative goal statements.

Using broad based survey techniques, with carefully planned stratified sampling procedures assuring that no group is underrepresented, these tentative goals are then circulated for reaction. Information obtained in this way helps determine how closely the statements correspond to local expectations for the schools. The results are used to revise and formalize a set of educational goal statements to guide systemwide educational planning.

Before adoption of the goals, generally by the local Board of Education, the clean slate process calls for their distribution in finalized form to participants involved in the earlier survey. At this time, respondents' views are determined concerning the relative importance of various goals. The data gathered in this last step provide a valuable information base for decision makers. The clean slate approach enables them to consider the expressed expectations of various client groups in making decisions about goals, programs, and resources.

The Predefined or Canned Process

A second well known approach to setting educational goals relies on predefined or canned lists of possible goal statements. In this approach prepared sets of goal statements, ranging in number from eighteen in the Phi Delta Kappa kit to over one hundred in the Center for the Study of Evaluation materials, are assigned ratings by selected individuals. The rating procedures may be carried out at meetings involving a sample of teachers, students, parents and other participants. Other strategies for securing ratings of the specified goals can be used, including card sorting or survey techniques. Rating the goal statements involves assigning numbers to indicate the degree of importance attached to each educational outcome. Formulas are used to compute averages and establish ranks or priorities. In using these formulas, it is customary to assign various weights to the views of different client groups, based on a predetermined judgment of whose opinions should be given greatest emphasis.

The predefined or canned approach relies on goals and activities that have been specified in advance by an external source. This approach can be completed in a much shorter time span than the clean slate approach described earlier. Although time may be saved by using a canned approach, there is far less commitment to the goals because of the limited involvement of the client groups.

The Modified or Combination Process

To better reflect the local situation while retaining some of the efficiency of the predefined approach, a number of districts have used a modified or combination goal setting process. It is possible, for example, to develop a set of outcome statements drawn from local curriculum documents and other published sources. These statements can be used to develop a survey instrument that, in general, reflects the current curriculum. The modified approach takes into account locally developed expectations and partially avoids the time consuming activities associated with using the blank sheet process. Instead of working from open ended responses the modified approach is based on specific local outcome statements.

These advantages are more likely to occur if the survey form is referenced to the status study information. The instrument may include a large number of outcome statements, but it should not be too lengthy. It should be distributed to a wide range of respondents. After receiving reactions from a representative sample of population subgroups, a team or advisory group can help cluster appropriate items into general goal statements. A follow up survey using the refined goal statements may be conducted to help establish local priorities. If this is not feasible, data from the initial survey can be analyzed to determine the major unmet needs identified by various groups of respondents.

The modified or combination approach has sufficient flexibility to be useful in many different educational settings. Ample time needs to be allowed for careful survey preparation, distribution, and analysis. However, the number of mailings or other community contacts will be much smaller than those needed with the clean slate approach. When planning the goal setting process, it is very important to establish clear communication and generate as much local support and understanding as possible for the educational program. Thus, the costs of staff and community involvement should be weighed in relation to the expected payoff from the goal setting activities.

The Role of Needs Assessment

The approaches described in the preceding section provide a range of options for establishing educational goals and priorities. These approaches vary in terms of: staff and public participation, time and cost considerations, and other important dimensions. Each can be combined in some way with appropriate needs assessment strategies.

Educational needs were defined as the differences between actual and desired performance. Needs assessment, a term which has been applied rather haphazardly in recent years to cover a raft of widely different activities, simply means a process for determining needs that may exist. A determination of the relative importance of identified needs may also be a part of the needs assessment process.

It has been emphasized that goals should emerge from the identification of existing needs. Thus, needs assessment is seen as a process which should precede the establishment of educational goals. This position does not rule out the inclusion of needs assessment activities in the goal setting process itself. However, it is important that the procedures used to measure existing needs be compatible with the basic assumptions held about goals and effective goal setting practices.

If a school system is using a limited participation process for establishing goals, such as the committee or task force approach or one of the canned programs, the needs assessment activities may not have a high level of client involvement. Consideration can be given by designated individuals or groups to such data sources as: standardized test results, records of report card grades, and employment or post secondary education patterns of graduates. Information acquired from the selected data sources can then be compared with either the predefined goal statements or with other bases for judgment. These may include professional association standards or information about similar school systems. As a result of these comparisons, areas can be determined where expectations exceed performance (unmet needs), are surpassed by current performance (met needs), or are consistent with desired performance.

In cases where the preferred goal setting process involves wider participation by various groups, needs may be identified quite differently. Perceptions of staff members, students, parents, and others regarding current levels of performance or accomplishment can be emphasized. Questionnaires can include opportunities for respondents to comment on present performance as well as the perceived importance of all educational outcomes. Use of test results and other data sources would be optional in this needs assessment strategy. Identification of met and unmet needs would be based primarily on the discrepancies between current perceived status and reported expectations of those concerned with the educational programs.

Needs assessment, then, may or may not be done in conjunction with goal setting activities. The important point is that goals should be based on the most accurate and up to date information about existing educational needs. Further, needs assessment techniques can provide valuable data for reviewing and regularly evaluating stated goals. Many curriculum workers know how essential it is to be aware of changes in community values, expectations, and feelings of satisfaction with the local schools. Needs assessment processes can help educators be aware of the perceptions held by all important client groups of the schools.

A Design for Goal Analysis

The focus of this section is on the analysis activities which lead to the establishment of desired educational goals. The goal analysis will be more effective when it is preceded by a status study which describes current conditions. When status information is available, those responsible for the development and evaluation process know whether or not written goals exist for the program being studied. They are also aware of the important events which led to formulation of the current goals, including when the major goal setting activities took place.

Once status descriptions have been prepared, the analysis process focuses on determining the appropriateness and quality of current goals. Frequent referencing of status information occurs as decisions are made about steps which should be taken to strengthen existing goals. If necessary, additional data about present goals, philosophy, needs, and priorities may be sought to answer particular analysis questions.

It is important to keep in mind that the specific goal improvement activities used may vary considerably according to the scope of the program. Goal improvement for a districtwide curriculum would be much more complex than for a kindergarten program at a particular school. Large scale development and evaluation programs often require the use of surveys and other data gathering techniques that facilitate contact with a wide audience. Formal committee structures may be needed in order to efficiently manage goal analysis or goal setting processes. Variation in the size or type of program being considered does not necessarily alter the basic approach to this crucial phase of development and evaluation.

Results of the status study can also be expected to affect the pattern of goal improvement activities. Curriculum developers and evaluators should generally avoid duplication of recent goal related activities. Even if the needs assessment or goal setting processes appear to have certain deficiencies it is usually wise to avoid creating hostility by engaging in activities likely to be perceived as redundant or time wasting. Plans for goal analysis can be devised to supplement or update the available data with some form of easily obtained information about current needs and expectations.

Several helpful techniques can be used in planning the goal analysis. Goals and philosophy statements can be reviewed and discussed by department or program level faculty groups. Advisory panels, including representatives of a broader range of concerned groups, can be asked to work with development and evaluation specialists in the goal analysis process. They can help screen existing statements or review items for proposed survey instruments.

If the task of screening and assessing goals seems to merit widespread participation students, teachers, and parents may be asked to take part. The respondents can be interviewed or surveyed to interpret present goal statements in their own words or to give other indications of goal clarity and meaningfulness. They may also be asked to assess the goals' importance and present accomplishment as part of a more extensive needs assessment or goal setting process. In cases where the status study reveals an absence of written goals or clearly indicates that those available are sketchy, outdated, or otherwise in need of revision, some form of goal setting process should be initiated. The goals which emerge from this process should themselves be analyzed to ensure that they represent a clear, comprehensive interpretation of expected educational outcomes.

Answers to questions similar to those listed below can be valuable in analyzing and improving program goals. The questions are based on criteria which have been found to be helpful in this phase of the development and evaluation process. Additional questions should be initiated to address points of special interest or concern in the local setting. The goal analysis process should help prepare responses to such questions as:

1. Do the goals reflect worthwhile and attainable educational outcomes?
2. Is a consistent set of educational beliefs or assumptions reflected in the stated goals?
3. Do the goal statements exhibit such desired intrinsic qualities as: clarity, focus on learner outcomes, and appropriate levels of generality?
4. Have priorities been established for the goals based upon identified needs?
5. Does a process exist for regular review and refinement of the goals?

When steps have been taken to reference the values of appropriate groups concerned with the educational program, as pointed out in Proposition A, the answers to questions 1 and 2 above are more likely to be answered affirmatively. Goals should help give direction and purpose to an educational program that takes into account local values and expectations. Priorities should be established so that resources can be properly allocated to achieve the important local expectations.

The advantages of clearly defined goals and priorities will be seen repeatedly as further improvement phases are described in the remainder of this book. These advantages are best realized when the goals and priorities are subject to periodic assessment so that timely responses can be made to changing client needs. Goal analysis should take place at regular intervals if the best possible set of educational goals is to be maintained as a basis for ongoing development and evaluation activities.

Relationship to Other Development and Evaluation Approaches

Virtually all leading curriculum development models begin with a goal setting stage. Tyler and Taba clearly established the importance of goals in guiding further phases of curriculum development. Their influence is still very much in evidence today. In some humanistic or experience oriented curriculum approaches, goals may have a diminished role in the development activities, but there are underlying purposes or assumptions which give direction to curriculum workers.

Evaluation models and frameworks exhibit a similar consistency in addressing goals or intended outcomes. Those who define evaluation as determining the extent to which performance is congruent with stated objectives are linked to goal referenced evaluative activities. Tyler and Hammond are well known supporters of this particular position.

Scriven and Stake extended the thinking about educational goals by stressing that the quality of those goals should be assessed by evaluators. This important concept has since been incorporated into most of the widely accepted evaluation models or frameworks. The initial stages of such models generally include varying degrees of attention to goal evaluation. For example, in Stake's model this occurs as part of antecedent evaluation, while Stufflebeam deals with goals in the phase known as context evaluation.

Development and Renewal Activities

1. Identify an educational program that you know about and find out as much as you can about how the goals were developed. Analyze the process used and recommend procedures that might have helped improve the process.

2. Discuss with one or more other persons the importance of making educational goals known to students, parents, staff members, and others. Propose strategies that could be used to make these groups more aware of the goals and to give them a better understanding of program purposes.

3. Assume the role of a curriculum worker involved with a committee charged with improving the K–12 science curriculum of a local district. Several members of the committee have expressed the view that goals tend to be statements that sound important but are seldom used productively. React to this viewpoint, presenting your response as you would share it with fellow committee workers.

4. Refer to appropriate readings to become more familiar with the ways that goal setting and goal evaluation are handled by different writers. Compare and analyze the approaches you have read about and identify the features you like or dislike about each goal setting process.

Bibliography

Hoepfner, Ralph et. al. *CSE/Elementary School Evaluation Kit: Needs Assessment.* (First in a five-part series). Boston: Allyn and Bacon, Inc., 1972.

Popham, W. James. *Educational Evaluation.* Englewood Cliffs, N.J.: Prentice-Hall, Inc., 1975.

Robertson, Neville and William Gephart. "Educational Goals and Objectives: An Assessment of the PDK Planning Model," CEDR, Vol. 7, No. 2, Summer 1974, pp. 12–15.

Saylor, J. Galen and William M. Alexander. *Planning for Better Teaching and Learning.* New York: Holt, Rinehart, and Winston, 1981.

Taba, Hilda. *Curriculum Development Theory and Practice.* New York: Harcourt, Brace and World, Inc., 1962.

Worthen, Blaine R. and James K. Sanders. *Educational Evaluation: Theory and Practice.* Worthington, Ohio: Charles A. Jones Publishing Co., 1973.

Chapter 5

Organizational Considerations in Development and Evaluation

Introduction

One important phase of the status study described in Chapter 3 is to generate information about organizational factors which influence the achievement of educational goals. Many times the goals of an organization are not being attained because inadequate consideration has been given to organizational processes and influences. Adjustments in the organization can lead to greater efficiency in accomplishing goals, especially when resources are limited.

Nearly all curriculum development and evaluation frameworks give considerable attention to needs assessment and goal setting activities. These approaches generally reflect the assumption that when educational goals have been properly formulated the next activity is to develop program content and materials. Certainly this seems to be a logical assumption. However, programs may be developed on this basis and then due to a variety of organizational influences or constraints cannot be successfully implemented.

Inadequate resources or a lack of clarity about responsibility for program implementation may interfere with goal attainment. These are just two of the many organizational influences which may affect short or long term program success.

It has become apparent as the field has matured that effective leaders in the area of curriculum must also be well informed about organizational improvement, evaluation and renewal. They must have a clear understanding about basic organizational processes and the effects of those processes on day to day operations. In addition to understanding the workings of an organization, curriculum workers must be prepared to give leadership to development and evaluation activities which will help the organization achieve its high priority goals.

In this chapter a basic plan for conducting development and evaluation activities that can increase the likelihood of successful program implementation is presented. The organizational considerations discussed here do not include all possible influences, but they can provide a sound basis for program planning. These considerations should also serve to stimulate further thinking about how organizational influences affect the curriculum.

Basic Concepts and Definitions

The earlier status study discussion refers to descriptions of organizational factors and influences. The organizational considerations which need to be dealt with include: all resources in the organization, the structural relationships, those processes that are basic to organizational functioning, and the programs which have been developed to carry out important educational goals. Each of these considerations is explained more fully in the following material.

Resources

Educational organizations depend most heavily on their human resources. Approximately eighty percent of all financial resources available to education are expended to employ the personnel who help the schools function. It is essential to understand how to best utilize these human resources. Perhaps the most important human resource is the competency to carry out assigned functions. Appropriate personnel selection and evaluation processes will help assure the adequacy of the human resources.

Physical resources are necessary if organizational goals are to be achieved. Even the most competent personnel cannot respond adequately to expressed needs if they do not have the necessary facilities, equipment and material. Financial resources must be adequate to carry out staffing expectations and to provide the necessary equipment and materials. It is most important for the financial resources to be sufficient so that adequate time can be allocated for carrying out essential organizational activities.

Time is also a critical resource for all educators. The proper allocation of time is necessary if programs are going to be successful. Even if sufficient time has been allocated, those responsible for programs must see that this valuable resource is properly used.

Structure

Organizations are, of course, very complex entities. The arrangement of the resources of an organization may be thought of as its basic structure. If the important organizational goals are to be achieved, the resources must be properly organized.

Organizing the human resources may be the most challenging task facing leaders in education. One major activity designed to improve the arrangement of the human resources is the development of position descriptions. Unfortunately this activity has often been given low priority in the organizational improvement process. In fact, many educational organizations are operating without any clear delineation of functions, roles, authority, and responsibility.

When position descriptions are properly developed, they clarify the key functions for each person's area of responsibility. The position descriptions also help specify the roles necessary for developing and executing those policies which help the total organization function properly.

Position descriptions should carefully delineate the authority as well as the responsibility for all key functions that have been specified for each position. Very often responsibilities are specified without adequate clarification about the level of authority needed to meet the expectations of the assignment. Carefully developed position descriptions are necessary if human resources are to be effectively organized to achieve important organizational expectations.

Serious attention must also be given to the arrangement of the organization's financial and physical resources. One process for determining the appropriateness of financial and physical resource allocation is to use the high priority goals as a frame of reference. In successful organizations, available resources are efficiently organized to achieve the most important goals. In these organizations relationships between goal achievement and resource allocation are clear. Processes for review and adjustment help staff members respond to changing goals, new program needs, and fluctuations in funding levels.

Organizational Processes

There are several important processes that critically influence how well the organization functions. These processes are closely related to the major leadership responsibilities and activities of the organization. For example, the communication process affects all personnel in the organization. Many organizations rely almost entirely on communication procedures which cause information to flow from the top levels of the hierarchy down through the other levels of the organization. There must be an opportunity for vertical communication up through the organization as well as laterally to other units if the communication process is to be effective.

The decision making process also directly affects day to day operations in the organization. It should be clear to all personnel which decision making strategies will be used to solve the wide range of problems faced by those working in a complex organization. How important decisions are made has been shown to be an important influence on the level of commitment demonstrated by members of the organization.

The processes used to allocate resources have a significant impact on goal achievement. Staffing procedures as well as financial and physical allocations help determine which goals can be effectively achieved. Resource allocation has a major impact on organizational effectiveness and must be understood by those involved in program development and evaluation.

The planning process must also be carefully developed and implemented on a systematic basis. How well all personnel plan their work has a major bearing on individual and group performance. Both short term and long range planning should be considered high priority activities at all levels of the organization.

Ongoing and systematic renewal activities are necessary for both individual and organizational development. The renewal process should be aimed at developing and improving the skills, knowledge, and understandings of all members of the organization. When renewal is given a high priority, individual performance is very likely to improve and a renewing attitude can be created throughout the organization.

There are, of course, other important processes which influence how organizations function. Those discussed in this section represent the most critical of these processes and require careful consideration as program development and evaluation activities proceed.

Programs

Agreed upon goals should give direction and purpose to all activities conducted by those in the organization. Clearly, resources are needed to support each of these ongoing activities. Available resources should be structured or arranged so that program goals are most likely to be achieved. Generally, related clusters of goals can be identified that are compatible with the various programs offered by the school or system. A program can be defined as a set of goals and specific objectives with the resources necessary to reach the objectives. Programs should be developed to achieve all major goals of the organization, with each program addressing one or more broad goals. The way programs are structured varies in different schools and systems. For example schools with self-contained classrooms structure their programs differently than departmentalized schools. Other structures include: unified studies, fine arts programs, and enrichment programs. Whatever the structure there should be a clear relationship to program goals and system goals.

Programs in educational organizations include those needed to achieve important educational goals as well as those necessary to carry out other essential services such as transportation and food services. The mathematics program, for example, consists of a set of instructional objectives and the resources necessary to fulfill general goals in that subject area. Programs such as transportation may have objectives which are not directly related to the instructional program. However, getting students to and from school safely is a very important goal that depends on adequate resource allocation.

It should be apparent that the resources available to an organization limit the number of goals that can be expected to be given full attention. Thus, all programs should be carefully screened using the goals as a frame of reference. Decisions can then be made about the need for new or existing programs and the appropriate resource allocation for each program.

Propositions about Organizations

The assumptions held about the nature of educational organizations and their roles in development and evaluation influence curriculum workers involved in improvement activities. If organizations are viewed as being unnecessary bureaucracies that interfere with individual creativity and freedom, there may be very little attention given to the organization in the development and evaluation process. This could lead to the omission of critical activities that could generate information about the influence of organizational resources, processes, structure, and programs.

Each organization is unique. While similarities are likely to exist in areas such as the type of line and staff relationships, the character of each educational organization reflects local needs and influences. Although these local factors must be considered, there are also several general premises that should merit attention in any program improvement effort. These premises are the basis for the philosophy presented in this chapter about how organizations should be viewed in development and evaluation programs. The propositions summarized below are based on assumptions and findings about organizations that can give direction to program improvement efforts. They are consistent with the development and evaluation activities presented in the following sections.

A. **Participants in an organization should place a high priority on developing unity of purpose.** When people work together in an organization it may be assumed that they are attempting to achieve common organizational goals. Ideally, that is what should be taking place. All too often that is not really the situation. Many times the participants are working at cross purposes or expending their energies in different directions. There are a set of conditions which can help those in an organization develop the unity needed to help them work toward a common set of purposes.

The goals and philosophy held by participants must be viewed as the most important condition affecting their chances of achieving a general unity of purpose. As discussed in Chapter 4, it is critical for all participants to be involved or represented when the goals and philosophy for the organization are developed. If all concerned groups have an opportunity to be productively involved, it is much more likely that they will make a commitment to the goals that are generated by the process.

How well the participants understand their roles and responsibilities in the organization is another important condition affecting unity of purpose. The development of position descriptions can be an important process for improving organizational unity. If the position descriptions are developed by the persons in each position and then clarified and agreed upon at the next higher level of the organization, individual commitment to specified roles and responsibilities is increased. When the position descriptions are written and handed down to those in the lower levels of the organization, there is less chance that the commitment necessary for a high level of goal achievement will be obtained.

The organizational processes discussed in the previous section can also have considerable influence on the degree of unity. If the communication process does not allow for feedback from all levels of the organization, a negative condition can be created which is likely to impede efforts to achieve important goals. A similar condition exists when decision making processes do not provide for adequate participant involvement. All important organizational processes should allow for appropriate participation by school or system personnel. This helps develop a positive set of conditions that can unify the efforts of those attempting to achieve the organizational goals.

B. **Participants in an organization should have the opportunity to achieve their personal goals as well as those of the organization.** The importance of setting and achieving organizational goals has been stressed. This cannot be ignored if the organization is to be healthy and productive. Sound organizations will help the participants achieve their own goals. Numerous authorities regard this as basic to maintaining a high level of commitment to the organization.

When an organization is involved in a comprehensive goal setting process, participants should have an opportunity to express their expectations and aspirations. When this is done it is very likely that the organizational goals will reflect many of the individual expectations. This is one aspect of the personal goal fulfillment process. However, further action is needed so that individual goals can be clearly identified and achieved.

Each participant in an organization should identify several personal goals to be worked toward each year. These goals should be the basis for a personal yearly work plan. Annual work plans provide an opportunity for all personnel to make a written commitment to achieving personal as well as organizational goals. The development of the work plans also provides an opportunity for those working at different levels of an organization to become partners in the process of goal achievement.

Personal goals should be established on the basis of quality not quantity. Having three or four high quality personal goals to work toward is more meaningful than having a large number of goals that are impossible to achieve or, conversely, are at such a low level that their achievement does not improve the quality of personal or professional life.

When personal goals are identified they should be realistic in terms of the resources available to carry them out. There may appear to be many constraints that interfere with successful goal achievement. Sometimes these constraints are real and sometimes they are imagined. By stating personal goals, presenting them in a formal work plan, and reviewing them with appropriate supervisory personnel, clarification can be reached about the potential opportunities for personal growth and development.

C. **Even though there are formal hierarchical relationships basic to organizational structure, it is possible to capitalize on the capabilities of all participants.** The structure of an organization should be flexible enough to allow for maximum utilization of all human resources. The position has often been taken that a formal organizational structure does not permit individuals to use their best abilities. There are processes which can be used to neutralize the potential negative effects of the formal structure.

Perhaps the most crucial factor in human resource management is the philosophy exhibited by the school or system leadership. When leaders sincerely believe that knowledge and creativity are found in a very limited group there tends to be very little commitment to the development of all personnel in the organization. On the other hand, leaders who sincerely believe that all members of the organization have competencies that are important and necessary to the organization tend not to allow the formal structure to interfere with the proper utilization of those competencies.

Several positive actions can take place when a philosophy supports the use of all human resources in the organization. One strategy involves providing for work enlargement within the formal structure. This process is based on the premise that all personnel can gradually assume more responsibility for the activities associated with their assignments. For example, school principals can be responsible for developing the staffing patterns of their schools so as to best meet the needs of each particular unit. The patterns they create may not follow a formula which has been developed for an entire system. Work enlargement should be seen as a means for promoting independence and personal creativity throughout the organization.

Action can also be taken to give teachers the opportunity to use their best skills and competencies as they work toward achieving the curriculum and instruction goals. They should make decisions about the strategies and materials which would be most appropriate to use on a day to day basis. Enlarging their work includes opportunities for involvement in decision making about all policies and regulations which affect their organizational expectations. Teacher work enlargement should not be restricted to classroom activities. There are many teachers with special skills that can be used to improve the total organization. Some schools have had teachers help other teachers develop new skills and competencies. This concept can be expanded to better utilize teacher talents throughout all levels of the organization.

D. **Organizations must be self renewing entities.** There has been considerable attention given to problems that seem to escalate as organizations mature. New schools typically start out with a spirit of energy and vigor. As schools grow older and their enrollments and resources begin to decline the participants are faced with different problems and challenges. Maintaining a commitment to the goals of an organization is especially difficult when there are fewer resources available to accomplish the goals.

The motivation necessary for all personnel to strive to excel can often be generated by providing the opportunity for them to use their best abilities in long range improvement programs. It is an important challenge for organizational leaders to engage in long range planning when it may appear more expedient to devote their energy to maintenance activities. Organizations tend to deteriorate and decay if a commitment is not made to systematic, long term improvement activities. This is especially true in educational organizations where human resources are central to success. Product oriented organizations tend to be as concerned about their mechanical or physical resources as they are about their personnel.

Educational organizations become self renewing only when individuals in the organizations believe that self renewal is an essential factor in their personal well being. This belief must be basic to the thinking that goes into their yearly work plans. It has been pointed out earlier that individuals should be able to achieve their goals while at work. Every work plan should include a personal renewal or development goal for the year. When individual renewal goals are achieved there is a strong likelihood that the organization will become more vigorous and dynamic.

Self renewal does not need to be thought of as a process which will cause a great deal of disequilibrium. Unfortunately the rapid changes and numerous innovations that characterized education organizations during the past fifteen to twenty years resulted in some needless problems. Many of the problems could probably have been avoided if the goals of the institutions had been the primary basis for making changes rather than simply reacting to popular trends.

Individual and organizational renewal should be thought of as a process which will help keep the vigor and energy of the participants at a level necessary to accomplish high priority goals. Renewal can not be left to chance; it must be planned for on a systematic and long term basis.

E. **Organizations must have mechanisms for generating information to support feedback and decision making activities.** Opinions vary about the need for evaluation of performance and programs and the role of evaluation in educational organizations. The purpose of evaluation should be to make some assessment about the worth or value of programs or performance in the organization. The process of evaluation should generate information necessary for determining worth or value.

Evaluation should be seen as a positive process which can help to improve performance or the products resulting from organizational performance. The process of generating information should be a nonthreatening activity. If the information gathered for evaluation is used with great care the process can be regarded by participants as helpful and worthwhile.

The mechanisms used for generating information about organizational activities and outcomes should be carefully planned. They should not be used only when the organization is having problems or there is external pressure for change. Efforts to bring about lasting improvements in crisis situations are far less likely to succeed than those that are part of a long range development and renewal plan.

When organizational goals are developed, procedures for regular review and revision should be established. The mechanisms for conducting such a review need not be used every year but should be agreed upon so that they can be used when needed. The review process should provide for a regular and systematic screening of the goals in terms of changing local and societal needs.

The organization should have mechanisms that generate information to give helpful feedback about individual and group performance. These would include: regularly scheduled planning conferences, monitoring of day to day activities, formative or improvement focused feedback sessions, and annual summative conferences. Once again these processes should be well established and used on a regular basis, not just when there are problems in the organization.

Procedures for determining how well the organization is achieving its projected outcomes should be comprehensive enough to generate information about all important expectations held for the organization. Testing and assessment processes can determine how much students have learned about specific subjects. A wider range of information is needed to assess how the learnings have been applied and used after the students have left the school or district.

Mechanisms which generate information about various aspects of organizational activity are also helpful in planning renewal programs. Evaluation for improvement is most effective when there are opportunities to use the information generated by these activities to plan long range individual and organizational development programs.

A Design for Organizational Analysis

In order to analyze and improve the organization, information about the various factors discussed previously must be available. The status study can provide a substantial amount of helpful data concerning resources, structure, programs, and organizational processes. However, a review of the existing data base may reveal areas which could be more effectively assessed if additional information were gathered.

The design presented in this section for organizational analysis is not intended to be all encompassing. It should serve as a referent point for those interested in analyzing their own organizations. No attempt has been made to completely exhaust all of the possible strategies available for analysis activities. The suggestions should stimulate individuals to consider appropriate ways of analyzing their own unique organizations. The questions posed are examples that might be used for some organizations but which may not be appropriate for others. When an organization is to be analyzed, careful consideration should be given to the types and quantity of information needed. Decisions should also take into account how the data are to be used in analysis activities. By taking care to plan a design well suited to the local situation, a more efficient and effective organizational analysis can be conducted.

Analysis of Resources

There are three general types of organizational resources to be reviewed and analyzed. Human resources constitute the great majority of those resources available to educational organizations. Physical resources include all of the buildings, equipment, and material available to the organization. Financial resources include all monies available for the spending plan. This includes monetary resources available for materials, equipment and instructional supplies.

If a status study has been conducted much of the pertinent information about resources is likely to be available. Staffing formulas and procedures are generally accessible for review in handbooks, policy manuals, or other documents. It should also be possible to determine from written materials the background and preparation of all school personnel. Information about staff members' renewal and inservice activities should also be included. Data concerning these and other aspects of human resources are useful when analyzing and assessing how well people are prepared to carry out their present assignments.

Budget documents can be used to examine expenditures for student support. Per pupil expenditures can be very important in assessing the adequacy of instructional materials and equipment. Financial records can also indicate levels of support for: staff development and renewal, instructional aids and equipment, maintenance of the physical plant, and other functions involved in operating an educational program.

It is necessary to actually observe the physical plant and facilities to determine if they are adequate to carry out the desired educational program. Observations and visitations can be especially useful in assessing the adequacy of laboratory and shop facilities and other programs with special equipment or facility needs.

An analysis of resources generally requires a complete review of appropriate documents as well as observations or visitations planned to gather data about facilities and equipment. Interviews with selected personnel may also be helpful in this process. Questions which should be answered by these activities include:

1. Are there sufficient personnel available for all important assignments?
2. Are the personnel properly prepared for their assignments?
3. Does the organization support staff development programs to improve the competencies of their personnel?
4. What is the level of funding for instructional support on a per pupil basis?
5. Are there any deficits in support for instructional materials and equipment?
6. Are the physical facilities adequate for all programs designed to achieve the goals of the organization?

Analysis of Structure

Structure has been defined as the arrangement of resources to carry out the goals of an organization. It is especially important when analyzing educational organizations to carefully examine the arrangement and allocation of available human resources. Most schools have committed at least eighty percent of their financial resources to personnel.

A status study would reveal if there are position or job descriptions for all personnel. The analysis activities should focus on how well all personnel understand their organizational roles and responsibilities. If there are position descriptions they should be analyzed to determine how clearly the roles and responsibilities have been delineated.

Analysis of the position descriptions should answer questions about: line and staff relationships, policy responsibilities, key functions of all personnel, and the authority and responsibility each person has to carry out these functions. After the documents have been analyzed, interviews with selected personnel from all levels of the organization may be conducted to corroborate and clarify the written information. Organizational charts should also be analyzed to cross check information for the interviews and the position descriptions. Any discrepancies that become evident during the analysis activities should be carefully noted.

Policy manuals, board minutes, and administrative regulation manuals are other sources of data for the analysis of structure. These documents should be examined to determine if the actual workings of the organization are in harmony with formal organizational arrangements. There may be policies which circumvent the normal reporting relationships. When this happens the structure may have been changed without the knowledge of certain staff members.

The appointment of special committees, task forces, and project teams has at times caused major changes in reporting relationships and in the roles, responsibilities, and authority of certain staff members. School systems may have special committees of teachers and administrators assigned to important tasks and reporting directly to the board of education. These committees may have special authority which allows them to circumvent the superintendent and central administration. When this happens major structural adjustments have been made.

Questions which may be used to give direction to the analysis of structure include:

1. Are there written position descriptions which clearly define role, responsibility, and authority of all personnel?
2. Do the position descriptions match the perceptions of the personnel about their work?
3. To what extent are formal organizational charts consistent with the actual functioning of the organization?
4. Do written documents such as policy manuals and board of education minutes support the agreed upon structural relationships?

Analysis of Organizational Processes

There are many processes that may contribute to organizational goal attainment. Analysis activities should focus on those which appear to have the greatest influence on organizational health and productivity. As a minimum, the analysis should focus on the following processes: communication, decision making, planning, and renewal and development.

A document analysis can help establish the formal lines of communication. Reporting relationships from position descriptions and other written material can be used to identify and assess the expected communication flow. The document analysis should be used as a referent point for discussions about the effectiveness of the existing communication process.

Interviews with representative personnel are necessary to determine which communication patterns and modes are most commonly used. Written documents may indicate that communication flows vertically throughout the organization. There may also be documents which illustrate horizontal patterns of communication based on cooperative working relationships. Interviews can generate important information about the effectiveness of communication patterns within the organization.

The interview process can also generate important information about modes of communication. The use of memos or general announcements to communicate with personnel should be noted. Efforts should be made to determine how often face to face communication is used and for what purposes. It is important to know how frequently the telephone is used to communicate on a one to one basis within the organization. Interviews can also be used to determine how often large and small group meetings are held and their effect on the communication process. Every attempt should be made to determine the purposes and frequency of all communication modes used in the organization, including the informal communication networks that are important to most organizations.

Decision making patterns and modes also need to be examined and analyzed. Document analysis can provide initial information about decision patterns used to arrive at policies, rules, and regulations. It is usually possible to determine the extent of involvement of appropriate personnel in the decisions which give direction to major activities of the organization. Minutes of board meetings and other important groups and committees can be used to determine the general patterns of decision making.

Interviews with representative personnel can generate important information about how often various decision processes are used. The decision processes that should serve as a focus for the interviews are: unilateral decision making, consensus decision making, and majority voting. Interview data should also help determine if the decision modes used for important long term changes are distinct from those used for immediate and less significant activities. In addition, it is important to determine how well the personnel understand the decision processes that are actually used to solve organizational problems. Conversations with staff members may reveal that not all personnel are fully informed about how important decisions are made.

A document analysis can be most helpful in determining the extent of formal planning done to achieve short term and long range organizational goals. The presence or absence of written plans is an indicator of the organization's commitment to the planning process. Planning documents should have information which includes: major goals, activities to carry out the goals, resources needed, time frames and target dates, and specific responsibility assignments.

Interviews with selected personnel will determine if written plans are being carried out. The degree of commitment to the plans may be clarified through the interview process. Information from the interviews can also be used to assess whether appropriate persons have participated in the planning process. Findings from the document analysis and interview data often serve to indicate the impact that planning activities have on organizational functioning.

A review of selected documents can identify the development and renewal expectations for the organization. Appropriate financial or personnel documents can give information about the relationship of the reward system to renewal expectations. Findings concerning the resources available for organized staff development programs are also indicative of the perceived importance of the development and renewal process.

Interviews with representative personnel can contribute to the analysis by clarifying the priority given to development and renewal programs within the organization. Personal interviews are often an excellent way to determine individual commitment to personal and organizational improvement. The adequacy of resources, including time, to carry out development and renewal programs can be assessed on the basis of data obtained through the interviews and document analysis.

There are numerous questions which can be used to give direction to the analysis of organizational processes. Examples of such questions include:

1. What are the formal communication patterns in the organization?
2. How congruent are the formal communication patterns with day to day operational communication patterns?
3. What communication modes are used most often and do they effectively achieve their purposes?
4. What decision making patterns and modes are most frequently used?
5. Are current decision processes leading to timely, appropriate resolution of problems and issues?
6. Do the personnel understand how important decisions are made?
7. Is there a formal planning process to achieve short term and long range goals?
8. How well has planning been used to achieve high priority goals?
9. Does the organization have a demonstrated commitment to development and renewal programs?

Analysis of Programs

When overall curriculum improvement is being sought by schools or systems, all programs developed to carry out organizational goals should be included in the analysis activities. Attention should be paid to those programs associated with educational goals as well as those that are often viewed as support programs. In this way, curriculum workers are more likely to recognize the effects of various programs on one another. When a broad view of program relationships is obtained, decisions about needed improvements can be based on a clear understanding of areas in which programs compete for resources, complement each other in reaching important goals, or exhibit duplication of effort.

A document analysis is an important process for identifying all possible programs in the school or district. After all programs have been identified, each program should be carefully analyzed. The analysis activities should include: identifying the major goals, identifying the resources available, and determining those with the responsibility and authority for the programs. After the programs have been analyzed they should be reviewed in terms of the stated organizational goals. This review should depict the relationship of each program to the goal statements. Relationships between programs should also be identified.

Interviews with selected personnel can be used to clarify the general understanding about the role and scope of existing programs. The interviews can also be helpful in determining the perceptions different personnel hold about the relative priority of each program. Those being interviewed can contribute information about those programs which they feel should be reduced or eliminated as well as those programs which seem to merit greater emphasis to accomplish high priority goals.

Questions that may be used to guide the program analysis activities include:

1. Are the programs adequate to carry out the important agreed upon goals?
2. Are the programs clearly stated and described?
3. Do all programs relate to the goals of the organization?
4. How are the programs organized or structured?
5. Do some programs have higher priority than others? If so, do they relate to the higher priority goals?
6. Are there programs which are redundant?
7. What changes, revisions, or additions are needed so that programs will be consistent with the goals?

Analysis of Organizational Characteristics

Although the activities described in the preceding sections deal with the major focal points for analyzing an organization, several additional questions need to be answered. It is true that since each organization is unique it would be inappropriate to expect all organizations to have exactly the same characteristics. However, the propositions presented about organizations imply the need to pose several additional questions as part of the analysis process.

The activities used to analyze organizational structure and processes will at the same time yield information about unity of purpose in the organization. For example, as involvement in important decisions is studied it is possible to infer the commitment and unity that personnel have in reaching important educational goals. Similarly, analysis of development and renewal processes can provide helpful indicators concerning the extent to which individuals are able to attend to personal as well as organizational goals. It has been found that a healthy organization is often characterized by activities which support personal goal achievement.

Organizations that capitalize on the best abilities of their personnel tend to be more effective in achieving institutional goals. The analysis of structure and processes will help provide information about this important organizational characteristic. Teachers and administrators who feel that they have opportunities to use their best abilities while at work tend to have a high level of commitment to the organization.

One of the most important characteristics of a healthy organization is the attention given to improving performance through ongoing feedback and evaluation processes. Positive personnel evaluation depends on clear expectations and agreed upon organizational goals. Procedures used to monitor and give feedback about performance should be consistent with the organizational structure and processes. When these factors are in harmony the motivation to achieve common goals is enhanced.

Questions to generate information about the characteristics of the organization may include:

1. Do the participants demonstrate sufficient unity of purpose to achieve the organizational goals?
2. Are there adequate opportunities and resources available for personal renewal programs?
3. Do the personnel feel that their best abilities are utilized by the organization?
4. Is there a comprehensive evaluation program designed to help improve performance?

Relationship to Other Development and Evaluation Approaches

Although most major evaluation frameworks imply the need for organizational evaluation, very few have given specific attention to this phase of the evaluation process. Perhaps the most helpful information related to this area of concern can be found in the Program Planning and Budgeting Systems which were quite popular during the late 1960's and 1970's. The PPBS format does give attention to structural and organizational considerations.

Hammond's objectives based evaluation framework identifies the important institutional variables which should be considered by those responsible for program evaluation. His framework can be used as one screen in determining the comprehensiveness of a design for organizational analysis.

Stufflebeam also gives some attention to structure in the Input phase of his CIPP model. His work can assist those who are concerned about the decision process in relation to program alternatives and options.

Although other evaluation theorists have given some general direction to the organizational analysis process, very few specific guidelines have been suggested. Those who developed the Individually Prescribed Instruction (IPI) program have identified several questions which are useful in determining the relationship of a plan to the stated project goals. Their work has given direction to several questions used for organizational analysis.

The concern about the organization and its structure expressed in this chapter goes far beyond other development and evaluation approaches. There are many instances where all program components seem to have been well developed but could not be implemented due to inadequate or inappropriate organizational structures and processes. Development and evaluation activities related to organization should help to assure that every attempt has been made to utilize all resources effectively and to ensure high quality educational programs for the students being served.

Development and Renewal Activities

1. Gather appropriate information to become more familiar with the organizational features of an educational program of your choice. Pose at least four questions that would generate helpful information for analyzing each aspect of the organization: resources, structure, organizational processes, and programs. Develop strategies for collecting data to answer these questions in the specific situation you have identified.

2. Hold a discussion with several other interested persons concerning the ways that individuals can be given opportunities to achieve both personal and organizational goals as members of educational systems. Consider how closely the present status matches desired conditions in organizations with which you are familiar. Discuss effects likely to occur when opportunities for goal attainment are not present.

3. Conduct an informal analysis of your own skills in such key areas as communication, planning, and decision making. Consult additional references to strengthen your understanding of one or more of these important organizational processes. Develop a set of guidelines based on your readings that will be helpful to keep in mind as you continue to expand your knowledge and skills.

4. Write a work plan for the coming year that includes the major goals you would like to achieve, including several professional goals and at least one personal goal. Include major activities planned to carry out the goals, resources or support needed, plans for monitoring progress, and intended evaluation of goal achievement. Discuss your work plan with at least one other person who can give feedback for improving the plan. If you do not currently hold a position in an educational organization, focus your plan on goals related to your present role.

Bibliography

Lindvall, C. M. and Richard C. Cox. *Evaluation As a Tool in Curriculum Development: The IPI Evaluation Program.* American Educational Research Association Monograph Series on Curriculum Evaluation. Chicago: Rand McNally and Company, 1970.

Planning, Programming, Budgeting System Manual for State of California School Districts. California: Peat, Marwick, Mitchell and Co., 1970.

Popham, W. James. *Educational Evaluation.* Englewood Cliffs, N.J.: Prentice-Hall, Inc., 1975.

Worthen, Blaine R. and James K. Sanders. *Educational Evaluation: Theory and Practice.* Worthington, Ohio: Charles A. Jones Publishing Co., 1973.

Annotated Bibliography

Gardner, John W. *Self-Renewal.* New York: Harper and Row Publishers, 1974. A comprehensive view of growth, decay, and renewal, both of societies and the individual is presented. Renewal depends in some measure on motivation, commitment, conviction, the values people live by, and the things that give meaning to their lives.

Chapter 6

The Operations Phase of Development and Evaluation

Introduction

School personnel usually feel quite familiar with activities that occur at the operations level of curriculum improvement. School systems have often begun their development and evaluation processes with activities related to the day to day workings of the curriculum. It is typical for teacher committees to be organized to develop curriculum guides or select texts and other materials. Procedures have been developed to adopt new courses, change instructional approaches, or introduce new testing practices.

The failure to place operational activities in the context of a systematic improvement process has often led to fragmented, inefficient development programs. Curriculum committees have tended to be formed in response to "crises" or pressures for change. Their work has often lacked coordination with similar activities in other grades or subject areas. The need for instructional improvement has often been responded to by providing workshops to meet some presumed teacher needs. Further, administrators have seldom received the help needed to develop their skills as curriculum and instruction leaders. The most successful curriculum development and evaluation activities occur when care has been taken to prevent these problems.

An overall strategy to strengthen the improvement process includes: developing an awareness of current status, establishing appropriate goals, and analyzing organizational factors likely to affect the success of any proposed changes. Agreement on important educational goals and ways to improve organizational functioning can contribute significantly to the smooth, efficient operation of the educational program.

The analysis and refinement of curriculum operations is a complex and challenging phase of the development and evaluation process. There are usually a large number of classrooms and other instructional settings to study. Within each one, there are innumerable human interactions that can affect curriculum implementation. Curriculum workers have begun to gain greater sophistication in analyzing classroom processes. By utilizing current teaching/learning research, they can significantly improve the ways that planned programs are put into operation on a day to day basis.

Many school districts are currently faced with unwieldy, overloaded curricula. Additional subjects or special programs have been added through the years. In the current situation developers and evaluators cannot afford to focus solely on one program. At least some attention should be paid to the workings of related areas of the curriculum and how they affect each other.

The operations phase typically requires a greater investment of time and human resources than other development and evaluation phases. However, it also has the potential for substantial payoff. Improved curriculum implementation, a stronger instructional program, and an efficient monitoring process can be realized through a well organized approach to operations analysis.

Basic Concepts and Definitions

The operations phase of development and evaluation is focused primarily on decisions related to curriculum and instruction. It is directly concerned with the day to day functioning of the educational program. Improving operations requires a careful analysis of the planned learning experiences and those which actually take place during instruction.

Definitions of the term, curriculum, abound in the educational literature. These definitions include some that interpret curriculum as a course of study or list of subjects offered. There are also a number of writers who define curriculum as the set of instructional objectives to be achieved by students. Another common definition of curriculum is considerably broader. In this interpretation, the curriculum includes all planned or unplanned school experiences.

The curriculum should not be limited to subject matter. It should include more than a specified set of instructional objectives. However, expanding the concept to include spontaneous events which occur in the cafeteria or on the school bus reduces the usefulness of the term. Curriculum should be clearly distinguishable from the general processes of education or daily living. The curriculum should include the planned experiences that students encounter in the learning situation. A school or system's curriculum is generally comprised of a number of programs such as language arts or vocational education. Each program is an arrangement of related objectives and the resources needed to achieve program goals.

In this interpretation of curriculum, goals are important guideposts. Goals have been defined as general statements of expected outcomes. These direction giving statements do not pinpoint time limits or measurement specifications. They represent broad but not vague indicators of important outcomes being sought in educational programs. Goals which are clear, appropriate, and stated in terms of learning expectations help give meaning and purpose to the school curriculum.

Instruction refers to the strategies and techniques used by the teaching staff to plan, implement, and evaluate the learning experiences included in the curriculum. A number of writers equate instruction with teaching, while others consider teaching just one of several instructional processes. There has also been a good deal of discussion about whether instruction should be treated as a part of curriculum or as a distinct and independent entity.

Teaching should be seen as a term that is more limited than instruction. Teaching refers to interactions between students and one or more other persons for the purpose of helping learning take place. Teaching may also involve interactions between students and appropriately designed materials. Methods of teaching include: lectures, discussions, question and answer sessions, demonstrations, simulations, inquiry or problem solving formats, and many other well known strategies. Activities such as establishing objectives and assessing learning outcomes are important aspects of instruction which are distinct from the actual teaching act.

Instruction is an essential process for translating the curriculum into action. It is a key consideration in any comprehensive approach to curriculum development and evaluation. Curriculum and instruction should function as mutually supportive dimensions of program operations.

A concept useful in working at the operations level is the instructional transaction. Instructional transactions consist of the specific objectives, activities, and materials necessary to fulfill the instructional goals established for a particular area of the curriculum. These transactions, carried out on a day to day basis, should collectively form a meaningful pattern of learning experiences. They should show clear relationships to the attainment of important educational goals.

Instructional transactions should be explicitly focused on student learning rather than on teacher behavior or subject matter. Objectives can play an important role in maintaining this desired focus. The diversity of opinion about how to state and use objectives is well known. Advocates of highly specific performance objectives recommend that each stated objective include such components as: success criteria, conditions under which the desired behavior is to occur, and materials or equipment to be used. Other educators propose that objectives can simply be general descriptions of the experiences learners are to have. These writers argue that learning is too personal and uniquely individual to justify stating performance objectives prior to teaching.

The definition of objectives as specific statements of intended learning outcomes is most consistent with the development and evaluation process presented in this book. These statements provide valuable indicators of students' success in achieving important educational goals. Objectives may either state or imply a time frame for completion and indicate a means for measuring their achievement. For certain types of instructional outcomes, particularly those which involve basic skills or competencies, detailed performance objectives may be quite useful. Learning outcomes which are more complex or developmental may call for instructional objectives which specify several observable indicators. These indicators are specific actions or results which would collectively suggest that the desired outcome has been achieved. Not every student may demonstrate every indicator, but patterns of related behaviors would be considered. This developmental form of objectives, advocated by Gronlund (1978), allows greater flexibility in accepting personalized indicators of success.

The term, content objectives, is used to denote statements that indicate what students are expected to learn. Process objectives specify what students will be doing while they attend to the content objectives. These two concepts have been especially helpful in instructional improvement activities. They direct attention to crucial learning processes as well as subject matter outcomes. Learning processes related to active participation, attention, and interaction with peers or teachers can have important effects on student achievement.

It has also proven helpful to include an analysis of objectives by domains and levels. Objectives should reflect a concern for outcomes in the cognitive (knowledge based), affective (feelings related), and psychomotor (skill oriented) domains. Failure to evaluate stated objectives may result in curricula which overemphasize the lower levels of cognitive learning. These outcomes, which include recall and basic knowledge, are generally easiest to specify and measure. They have tended to receive too much emphasis in curriculum development activities. On the other hand, such affective concerns as motivation, attitudes, and self concept have generally received too little attention by curriculum workers. Recent work by Bloom (1976) and his colleagues has helped promote increased awareness of the important relationship between affective characteristics and cognitive learning outcomes. According to their findings, curriculum workers need to carefully study the influence of students' entry characteristics, instructional quality, types of learning tasks, and time allotment for mastering objectives.

Propositions about Operations

In order to establish the clearest possible perspective for making decisions about programs, important assumptions and guidelines should be delineated. At the operations level, principles related to the day to day functioning of educational programs need to be stated. Basic notions concerning curriculum and instruction must also be examined. It is hoped that the ideas presented here encourage others to explore the premises they choose to accept concerning the operational aspects of development and evaluation. It is proposed that:

A. The day to day operation of the school or district should reflect a consistent and unifying focus on goal attainment. As ongoing activities and events are examined, concern for agreed upon educational goals should be evident. Personnel at all levels should be aware of high priority goals as they plan their work. This expectation applies equally to decision making about classroom instruction, staff development activities, evaluation procedures, and other key operations activities.

Experiences with a number of school districts have made it clear that observable indicators of commitment to goals can be identified. These indicators include: engaging in cooperative planning and problem solving, devoting time and energy to goal related tasks, and expressing or demonstrating concern for programmatic as well as personal needs. Another important indicator is the degree of congruency between planned curriculum guides and day to day classroom instruction. When the planned curriculum is consistently followed, it is much more likely that the educational outcomes will be in harmony with the expectations of the total staff, students, and community.

There are relatively straightforward steps that can be taken to give clear direction and purpose to educational programs. When general educational goals have been established, they should be used as a basis for developing or refining the curriculum framework. Schools or systems lacking an acceptable set of written educational goals should engage in goal setting activities similar to those described in Chapter 4.

After general educational expectations have been agreed upon, goals can be established for departments, instructional programs, or other appropriate units. If the overall educational goals of the school or system are seen as a first level (Level I), then program or department goals represent the second level (Level II) of intended outcomes. In a well-planned curriculum there are clear relationships between school or system goals and those established by departments or programs. Each important system goal (Level I) should be addressed by at least one department or program. At the same time, each important expectation agreed upon in departments or program areas should be related to at least one school or system goal.

Department or program goals should be established through discussions among all staff members associated with the program. Data sources for identifying appropriate goals can include such information as: written or oral feedback from current and former students, courses of study and other curriculum materials, reports prepared for the accreditation process, and recommendations of professional associations. The plan developed for establishing these goals should include a mechanism for screening them against school or system expectations. This activity is likely to suggest needed refinements in both sets of goal statements.

Once departmental or program goals have been agreed upon, course or unit goals can be established. This third level (Level III) of important learning expectations consists of statements which define the intended outcomes of each course or content/skill area. These statements give direction to the more specific objectives that are written in day to day instructional planning. The process for establishing course or unit goals should involve all members of the teaching staff who have some responsibility for the course. Cooperation and open communication are needed in order to bring about positive, lasting change in translating curriculum into daily operations.

Proposition B. Student learning should be the primary focus for day to day operations. In all activities associated with day to day operations, student learning must be the foremost consideration. Current practices should be regularly analyzed to ensure that tradition and convenience do not determine what takes place. Even if present practices seem to be producing satisfactory results, it is important to seek ways to ensure that students are gaining all they can from their school experiences.

Resistance to change has been a pervasive problem affecting curriculum and instruction. However, many educational organizations have experienced a very different problem with equally important consequences. Too often changes have been made for the wrong reasons. Pressure groups, educational fads, and funding opportunities are examples of factors that have influenced curriculum decision making. When such reactive, narrowly focused change becomes a pattern, it may be years before the full implications for student learning are discovered.

In order to accurately assess the effects of curriculum and instructional decisions on student learning, an understanding of learning theory is needed. Curriculum and instruction practitioners are most successful in operations level activities when they have developed a consistent set of beliefs about the learning process. Views held about how people learn affect the strategies used to: gain attention, determine readiness levels, encourage positive motivation, enhance retention of learned material, and help the learner apply knowledge and skills.

There are several important learning theories which offer alternative explanations of the learning process. Behavioristic learning theory places emphasis on the role of external factors in human learning. Stimulus, response, and reinforcement are key concepts in the behavioristic approach. The perceptual psychology or field theory approach takes a very different view of learning, emphasizing the role of personal experiences and individual characteristics. Learning and motivation are regarded as internal processes affected by a broad spectrum of mental, emotional, and environmental influences. A third major type of learning theory is the cognitive or information processing approach. The focus of this learning theory is on problem solving, memory, transfer, and other cognitive functions.

Curriculum and instruction practitioners who are familiar with these positions have a much better basis for operational decision making than those who lack such perspective. They are able to recognize the assumptions and principles implicit in curriculum materials or programs being considered for adoption. Programmed materials, individualized learning packages, and other educational programs and products should be screened in terms of their appropriateness for the learners being served and their compatibility with the learning approaches supported by the professional staff. Instructional strategies considered for classroom use should also be reviewed for consistency with established learning principles.

A sizeable body of important research on effective instructional strategies for learners of various age, ability, achievement, and socioeconomic levels has recently emerged. It is recommended that curriculum and instruction workers become more aware of these findings. Practitioners who keep up with the best current thinking about techniques which help students learn tend to reflect a renewing, growth oriented attitude toward their professional roles. As they use or encourage improved feedback strategies, better questioning techniques, and other research based practices, improved day to day operations and strengthened learning outcomes become apparent.

Proposition C. Instructional improvement should be a systematic, high priority operations activity guided by positive assumptions about teacher behavior. Instruction has been defined as a process which serves to translate the planned curriculum into a set of actual learning experiences. The instructional process includes important activities which take place before, during, and after the period of direct student involvement. Instruction is affected by a wide range of environmental factors, learner and teacher characteristics, and other school and home influences.

Research and experience have contributed to a rapidly expanding knowledge base about instruction. In order to refine and upgrade current skills, staff members with instruction related responsibilities should engage in regular improvement activities. It is also helpful to have a planned instructional monitoring process which can provide feedback about the effectiveness of day to day activities.

An important premise is that teachers and administrators want to be competent in their professional roles. When individuals resist change or display apathetic attitudes, it may be that they are actually insecure about their ability to change or improve. If this premise is accepted, the most appropriate approach may be to develop improvement strategies that will help satisfy basic human needs for competence.

One of the most effective ways to bring about this positive approach to motivating instructional improvement is through the ongoing classroom supervision process. As administrators visit classrooms and work with teachers on a regular basis, successful practices can be reinforced and those found to be interfering with student learning can be revised. The supervisory program offers an opportunity to monitor the implementation of the curriculum and to identify appropriate staff development activities for teachers and administrators.

A supervision process which focuses on the cooperative improvement of teaching and learning has achieved positive results in school districts across the country. This process, described by Bellon and Bellon (1982), is supported by several basic assumptions. They have assumed that teaching is a set of identifiable patterns of behavior which can be studied and improved through observation, analysis, and replanning. Emphasis is placed on the importance of mutual trust and collaboration as features of the supervisor-teacher relationship.

Building on these basic premises, a three part process has been developed. Prior to each scheduled observation, the supervisor and teacher hold a brief pre observation conference. This meeting gives the teacher an opportunity to explain the background, purposes, and procedures of the lesson to be observed.

The classroom observation is used to obtain a record of student or teacher verbal or physical behavior. Objective data collection techniques provide a basis for discussion and planning in the third phase of the process, the post observation conference. In this important conference, held as soon as possible after the observation, the supervisor and teacher have an opportunity to: review the classroom data, identify patterns of behavior which occurred, assess the patterns in relation to stated objectives, and engage in replanning for future instruction. Recommendations from the post observation conference typically include patterns to continue as well as those needing attention.

Whether this process or another approach is used, it is crucial that there be some form of operations monitoring. The process used should preferably emphasize a team effort to achieve mutually agreed upon goals. The maintenance of open communication is another important characteristic of an effective monitoring program. When these elements are combined with a demonstrated commitment by school leaders, major improvements are far more likely to be made and sustained.

Proposition D. Administrators at the building level have a major leadership role with respect to operations activities. Perhaps in no other phase of curriculum development and evaluation is the role of the school administrator more critical or less clearly understood. When curriculum and instruction are the subject of discussion, attention is usually focused on teachers and curriculum specialists. Principals are generally underestimated as leaders in curriculum implementation. They often do not realize the extent of their own potential or actual influence in this area.

The positive effects on teachers, students, and others that occur when a principal is committed to being a curriculum and instruction leader have begun to be recognized. A growing number of systems have acted to reinforce this positive commitment. For example, in one of the country's largest school districts the superintendent has developed a plan which emphasizes that principals will give leadership to instructional improvement in all of the schools. This has required some of the administrative duties typically performed by principals to be handled differently. The superintendent also recognized the need for staff development to help building administrators gain the skills required for their new leadership expectations. Because they have been given the support to improve their instructional leadership skills, the principals have demonstrated that they can be effective curriculum and instruction leaders.

There are specific steps that can be recommended to those seeking to strengthen curriculum and instructional leadership. It is critical that ample time be allowed for significant changes to be made. Multi-year plans are generally most realistic for implementing curriculum development and instructional improvement programs.

When a gradual, systematic approach to improvement is adopted, a major role of the building leader is to help maintain a sense of progress and accomplishment among staff members and important client groups. Actively involving teachers with strong leadership abilities in all phases of planning and training leads to increased credibility and support. The teachers help keep faculty members informed about the activities taking place and generate a stronger teacher commitment to the improvement process.

Having teachers and administrators learn and practice new skills together provides a valuable model for cooperative improvement efforts. For example, when a supervisory program similar to the one discussed in the preceding section is being installed, teachers and administrators can work cooperatively to develop the program. Administrators and teachers can practice conferencing and instructional analysis techniques with one another. As the new program gradually becomes operational, the cooperative training approach encourages a feeling of teamwork and commitment to the new program.

In addition to special development activities, building administrators should participate in staff development programs planned for the teachers. The most effective leaders have been found to participate actively in programs that are intended to improve the performance of their personnel. The leaders use these sessions to receive feedback that will help them improve their performance. At the same time, interpersonal relationships with all personnel can be strengthened.

The energy that leaders devote to strengthening interpersonal relationships with colleagues will benefit others in the organization. When administrators establish positive relationships with teachers, the teachers are more likely to develop favorable relationships with their students and colleagues.

A Design for Operations Analysis

The analysis of operations activities involves systematic attention to curriculum, instruction, and the many factors influencing their effectiveness. More of a school system's resources are devoted to operations level functions than to any other important set of activities. It is reasonable to expect that the process of analyzing day to day operations requires careful planning, adequate time, and sufficient resources.

In this section, a design for analyzing program operations is presented. The design is intended to serve as a framework or plan of action for those concerned with development and evaluation at the operations level. While the unique features of each situation will suggest additional questions and data gathering activities, the design can provide a starting point for this important task. Presentation of the design has been organized around several major themes drawn from the discussion of basic concepts, definitions, and propositions. These themes center on: curriculum, the plan or framework which gives direction to learning experiences; instruction, the process for implementing the curriculum; and related operations improvement activities.

The design for operations analysis is based on the assumption that multiple sources of data give a clearer and more accurate picture of programs in action than any single information source could provide. It is important to plan an appropriate combination of techniques for gathering information about curriculum and instruction. Emphasis should be placed on obtaining objective, factual data to reduce the likelihood of inaccurate or biased inferences. After appropriate data gathering procedures and instruments have been chosen, training must be provided in their proper use. Curriculum workers who shortcut these important tasks run the risk of decision making errors which may prove to be very costly and hard to detect.

An additional consideration in planning the operations analysis is to identify and collect only that information which is actually needed. When studying an area so rich in important information, it is tempting to collect a great deal of data from students, teachers, administrators, and others. If the information gathered is not essential to the development and evaluation program negative attitudes about the program may be created. In an era when people are subjected to many surveys and tests, a negative feeling may be generated by information seeking activities that are perceived as excessive.

It is helpful if the operations analysis design includes a set of key questions. These carefully chosen questions can focus the process on areas judged to be most important for studying and improving day to day operations. The questions generated for this purpose should reflect the unique features of the specific program. Results of the status study can highlight areas needing in depth examination at the operations level.

Strategies for conducting the operations analysis are discussed in detail in the following sections. A few general comments about the operations analysis team may be helpful prior to examining the specific strategies. In order to effectively carry out the operational analysis, a team approach is recommended. Questions about curriculum and instruction require knowledge about both content and process. Often expertise in a number of different subject areas and/or educational levels is required. In addition, the information handling and measurement needs of the operations analysis process make it important to have the assistance of someone trained in these areas.

Even if these diverse skills were found in one development and evaluation specialist, the scope and complexity of the operations analysis generally make it impractical for a single person to undertake the task. However, it should be possible to keep the size of the team reasonable in relation to the program being analyzed. Some tasks may be carried out by appropriate specialists on a contractual or service basis. Advisory groups or steering committees can also be helpful to the project team in a number of ways as the operations analysis proceeds.

Analysis of the Curriculum

Agreement on a set of important goals contributes to effective curriculum planning and implementation. Clear educational goals also help students, parents, and other clients understand the programs offered as well as the various program relationships that exist. An analysis of curriculum operations can begin with a review of the school or system level educational goals. As stated in Proposition A, efforts to achieve agreed upon goals should be evident in the day to day activities associated with carrying out the curriculum. A program may possess many fine, intrinsic qualities such as building on student interests or appropriate depth of content coverage. It must still demonstrate its contribution to achieving one or more important educational goals. Further, the goals agreed to have higher priority should be receiving greater attention than the lower priority goals.

General indicators of the harmony that exists between the curriculum and school or system goals and priorities include: the amount of emphasis placed on various types of academic and non-academic activities in the curriculum; the extent to which goals and priorities are referred to in communications related to the curriculum; and the level of awareness among students, faculty, and other groups about steps being taken to meet school or district goals.

Information concerning general indicators such as these can be obtained by several means. Documents can be analyzed for evidence of consistency with and reference to stated goals and priorities. In addition to actual curriculum guides or courses of study, suitable documents may include: minutes of board meetings; policy manuals; faculty and student handbooks; records of expenditures for various programs and services; information concerning assemblies, clubs, and activity programs; and school bulletins, newspapers, or other publications.

If further information is desired, administrators, faculty, students, and others can be surveyed. They can be asked how much attention is given to various types of educational activities. Their comments can be valuable in determining the relative emphasis placed on academic, cultural, social, athletic, recreational, and support or service programs. If needs assessment or goal setting activities have been conducted recently, this information may have been gathered and should be readily accessible. A status study would also be a valuable source of preliminary information for this phase of the curriculum analysis.

In addition to these general indicators of how effectively the curriculum addresses important educational goals, an in depth probe of the existing curriculum framework is needed. A well planned curriculum should show a clear transition from fairly broad outcome statements at the school or system level to major department or program goals, and then to more highly focused course or unit goals. The curriculum framework should provide the foundation for an articulated, carefully sequenced set of learning experiences for all students.

Analysis of the curriculum framework often reveals the need for several development activities. It is not uncommon to find that written curriculum materials are poorly developed or outdated. There may be a need to establish a written set of department or program goals, subsequently doing the same at the course or unit level. In designing a plan for this phase of curriculum improvement, opportunities should be provided for all faculty in each department or program area to discuss the relationships between their major goals and the overall school or system goals. Where discrepancies or areas of mismatch occur, department level goals may need to be revised. Recommendations may also be made for adjusting school level goal statements as needed.

Once the department or program goals have been analyzed for compatibility with overall educational goals, similar screening of course or unit goals should be conducted by appropriate faculty members. Results of the discrepancy analysis between course or unit goals and department or program goals should be presented for discussion by all members of the department. Recommended actions for dealing with discrepancies may include addition, deletion, or revision of specific goals, courses, or units of study.

In addition to the discrepancy analysis of curricular goals, steps should be taken to analyze all goal statements for intrinsic quality. As suggested in Chapter 4, any set of educational goals should be assessed in terms of: attainability, comprehensiveness, clarity, focus on learner outcomes, and importance or value. It is often helpful to use guidelines from professional associations and other appropriate resources as checkpoints in the review process.

To establish conditions for a productive operations analysis, ample time should be set aside for small and large group discussions, writing sessions, and presentation of reports. There should be clear guidelines for carrying out each activity, with support and assistance available when needed. The work of all groups or committees should be monitored to facilitate completion of assigned tasks.

Analysis of the total curriculum framework is best accomplished through the combined efforts of process and content specialists. Subject matter content must be carefully assessed in terms of its selection and organization. Content must be chosen and arranged so that learners can successfully achieve the desired goals. Subject matter specialists can help identify relationships across programs or courses. They may notice gaps or unnecessary overlaps in content coverage as well as opportunities for combined efforts. Persons with process expertise are needed to analyze the procedures used to develop and evaluate the curriculum framework. They should also conduct overall analyses of the goal statements and other curriculum components.

There are several questions which should be answered by engaging in the activities suggested above. The following are illustrative of the key questions one might use in the curriculum analysis process:

1. Is the curriculum framework consistent with established school or district goals and priorities?
2. Are the curriculum goals organized into a planned sequence?
3. Do course or unit goals reflect department or program goals?
4. Have all appropriate faculty members participated actively in the curriculum analysis?
5. Does a suitable process exist for revising curricular goals as needed?

Analysis of Instruction

Instruction has been defined as the process used to bring the curriculum into operation so that intended learning outcomes can be achieved. This close, complementary relationship between curriculum and instruction has important meaning for program improvement. Efforts to evaluate either curriculum or instruction in isolation must be viewed as incomplete.

Research and experience have shown that instructional practices can seldom be assessed on their intrinsic merit. Instructional patterns that "work" do so because they suit the intended goals and objectives. They are appropriate for the learners being served. When instruction is compatible with the curriculum framework, students see their learning experiences as having more meaning and direction. Improved motivation and learning are the likely consequences of this coherent, purposeful activity.

As Goodlad (1977) has recently observed, there are several perspectives from which any curriculum can be viewed. These range from the ideal or intended program to that which is actually experienced by each learner. There are often major discrepancies between the formal, planned curriculum and that which is implemented via instruction. When these occur, many important educational goals will not be met. Further, when sizeable gaps exist between the curriculum as taught and that which students perceive, learning will not reflect expectations. As emphasized in Proposition B, maintaining a focus on student learning is essential for effective program operation.

When planning an analysis of instruction the goals of the curriculum must be considered. The approach taken to fostering student growth, including underlying learning principles, must also be examined. Instructional analysis should be concerned with: the extent that instructional plans reflect stated program goals, the ways that learning experiences are sequenced, and the degree to which instructional approaches exhibit a consistent learning theory.

Information can be obtained by examining written plans in relation to curriculum documents such as goal statements, curriculum guides, and course syllabi. Interviews may also be conducted with selected teachers to determine their referent points for instructional decision making. By conducting preobservation conferences prior to classroom visitations, the evaluator can readily obtain important data concerning the curriculum context of each lesson, the teacher's awareness of student characteristics, and the strategies being used to adapt instruction to learner needs. If a balanced sampling plan is used, a series of these brief conferences can provide a very useful basis for an initial analysis of the "fit" between curriculum and instruction.

The process used to analyze instruction must not promote uniformity by applying inflexible criteria. It is important to recognize and reinforce the diversity which has been found to characterize the most effective teachers. Researchers conducting extensive studies of effective instructional practices have found that only the less successful teachers show a high level of similarity in their classroom behaviors. Teachers who are successful in helping students learn typically engage in a broad repertoire of instructional strategies to achieve their objectives.

Data collection techniques which preserve the rich texture of instructional behaviors are most desirable for the analysis process. Successful results can be obtained with written, narrative records, charts of actual student and teacher behavior, and other objective data collection techniques. These procedures, unlike most checklists or rating scales, do not call upon the evaluator to observe and make judgments simultaneously. To expect such dual recording and assessment is unrealistic in the busy, complex instructional setting.

The curriculum worker seeking to analyze and improve instruction should not focus on minimum performance criteria as the sole standard for judging success. Even the best teachers can improve their skills. They almost invariably welcome evaluation feedback which helps them refine specific techniques. The curriculum improvement process can be greatly enhanced by a classroom supervision program which provides objective information and feedback to all teachers in a supportive context.

Classroom observation data may be recorded in verbal logs that consist of narrative records of teacher and/or student statements. Behavioral charts such as classroom diagrams recording teacher and/or student movement, participation, or physical behavior can also be an important data source. These techniques make it possible to reconstruct classroom events with considerable accuracy. The instructional segment observed can be analyzed to identify behavior patterns. Among the many common patterns of recurring behavior are those involving questioning, reinforcement, control or management, and student participation. When the analysis of instruction includes this approach to data collection, there are no lists of predetermined behaviors to be sought in each lesson. The data used represent only what actually took place in the instructional setting.

Although one cannot say that particular behaviors are always effective, several important patterns do have substantial research support. Students' academic learning is generally enhanced by: thorough planning, appropriate allocation and use of learning time, clarity of objectives and expectations, and provision of ample feedback and correction. Assessment of instruction should be conducted by persons knowledgeable about these and other pervasive patterns. The combined judgment of content and process specialists is desirable when conducting a full evaluation of the instructional program. Teachers and supervisors can work together very productively to generate information about instruction that will be very important in the analysis activities.

In order to get an accurate picture of the current instructional program, the design for analysis should include an appropriate number of observations. A suitable variety of instructional settings should be visited. Observations should cut across grade levels, subject areas, or other applicable units of the overall program. As noted earlier, selecting a stratified random sample of classes is often needed to obtain a balanced overview. In addition to these systematic observations, it is often helpful to review plan books, analyze the texts and materials in use, and examine samples of student work. Each of these written data sources provides information about day to day instructional practices.

Interviews with students or simple written surveys can also provide valuable information for analyzing instruction. It is often important to determine student perceptions concerning key aspects of the teaching/learning process. Their responses can help clarify current levels of student involvement and motivation. Oral or written feedback from teachers, aides, librarians, guidance counselors, or other staff members may be useful in providing further data for this phase of development and evaluation.

When instructional transactions are being studied it is helpful to pose several questions to guide the analysis process. The questions that follow are examples of those that can be used to analyze and improve day to day instructional transactions:

1. Are stated instructional objectives consistent with course or unit goals?
2. Do the objectives represent appropriate levels and types of learning?
3. Are pre and post assessment techniques suited to the objectives and the learners?
4. Are the content and instructional materials appropriate for achieving desired learning outcomes?
5. Do the instructional methods fit the stated content and process objectives?
6. Are teaching and management strategies used to maintain the conditions needed for effective learning?
7. Is a systematic process used to assess individual and group progress toward curriculum goals?
8. Does an ongoing process exist for identifying and making needed changes in instructional practices?

Analysis of Operations Improvement Activities

The operations analysis cannot be considered complete without examining several related activities which influence the success of any educational program. These activities include: systematic instructional improvement, curriculum monitoring and revision, and staff development activities. It is unlikely that educational programs can achieve long term success if the staff does not make an active commitment to renew and refine professional skills, evaluate current performance, and plan for future growth. Leaders must be expected to model these patterns on a day to day basis, with personnel at all levels sharing the responsibility for improving program operations.

The design for operational analysis should include activities for determining the effectiveness of current supervisory practices, staff development opportunities, and curriculum improvement strategies. Information may be available from a status study concerning recent changes in curriculum or instruction. It is helpful to know how and by whom these changes were initiated and carried out. Data about the staff development and supervision or instructional improvement programs may also be available from earlier development and evaluation activities.

To supplement these initial data sources, a review of major operations improvement processes is recommended. Involvement of administrators as well as teachers in ongoing instructional improvement and staff development experiences should be determined. Procedures for identifying staff development needs and providing appropriate experiences to meet those needs should be studied. For example, it is important to determine how well staff development and instructional improvement activities support the attainment of personal and professional goals as well as school or system goals. In addition, program developers and evaluators need to analyze the attitudes that exist toward instructional improvement and related activities. As more is learned by curriculum workers about the teaching/learning process, instructional leaders at the classroom, school, or system level have a greater responsibility than ever to participate actively in improvement programs.

The most productive data collection strategy for this phase of the operations analysis may include a combination of self-report techniques. These include interviews, surveys, and attitude scales or opinionnaires. A sample of individuals who have initiated, participated in, and been affected by major changes in curriculum or instruction should be interviewed. This group can help provide a balanced perspective of the nature and effects of these activities. Interviews, surveys, or attitude scales can be used to determine how supervision, curriculum monitoring, and staff development activities are perceived by various groups. Discussions with selected staff members can also be helpful in determining steps presently being taken to meet personal and professional goals.

Self-report information can be supplemented by a variety of written data sources. Agendas or descriptions of workshops and other staff development activities are generally available for review. Curriculum documents developed in recent years, including materials prepared for textbook review processes or curriculum improvement efforts, should also be examined. Faculty handbooks, supervision and evaluation guidelines, and other pertinent documents are often helpful in this phase of operations analysis.

Assessment of existing improvement programs should be viewed as a basis for developing more effective development strategies. The design for operations analysis is more than a plan for studying and evaluating day to day activities. One of its major contributions can be initiating activities that will lead to ongoing feedback and improvement as the program continues to operate.

Relationship to Other Development and Evaluation Approaches

The areas dealt with in operations analysis have often been viewed as the core of curriculum development and evaluation. A great deal of activity has focused almost exclusively on the day to day workings of educational programs, virtually neglecting their organizational foundations and underlying assumptions. Most of the well known frameworks or models of development and evaluation reflect recent attempts to provide a more inclusive approach to the task of curriculum improvement. Each framework continues to recognize the importance of effective operations functioning for overall program success.

In Stake's judgment oriented evaluation framework, the term "transactions" is applied to the range of encounters among students, teachers, and materials in the instructional setting. Observation of these transactions provides data for assessing the congruency or match between intended and actual events.

While Stufflebeam adopts a somewhat different orientation to the evaluator's role, his CIPP model does include in the process evaluation component a concern for program functioning. Process evaluation, also a feature of the framework developed by Provus, provides regular feedback on program implementation. Process evaluation is regarded by both theorists as a way to anticipate and help to overcome procedural or operational difficulties.

Alkin, in a comparable vein, has proposed two stages in which operation related concerns are addressed. In the program implementation phase, process information is gathered and assessed. The phase designated "program improvement" provides data on the interim achievement of desired outcomes. This approach is consistent with the view expressed throughout this chapter that operations analysis activities should be designed to provide timely, helpful feedback for program improvement.

Clearly, the importance of the task and the range of areas which need to be analyzed make it essential that ample time be allotted for studying program operations. In most development and evaluation projects, this phase requires more resource support than other activities, particularly when there are numerous classroom observations. The resources set aside for operations analysis should be viewed as expenditures that will improve the entire educational program of the school or system. When operations improvements are initiated the benefits to student learning should be well worth the resources expended.

Development and Renewal Activities

1. Read *Classroom Supervision and Instructional Improvement,* 2nd Edition, by Bellon and Bellon to become familiar with a systematic, data based process for observing and improving instruction. Practice your conferencing and observation skills by arranging to sit in on several classroom lessons. Discuss your findings with several colleagues or peers.

2. Suggest several strategies or techniques useful for monitoring the effectiveness of curriculum implementation. Consider strengths and weaknesses of each. Apply the results of this analysis to an educational setting of your choice and make a preliminary assessment of the strategies currently used for this purpose.

3. Become acquainted with findings of recent research on effective instruction. *Instructional Improvement: Principles and Processes* by Bellon, Bellon and Handler would be a good starting point. Theme issues of Educational Leadership, Phi Delta Kappan, and other journals would be helpful, as would reports such as *Time to Learn,* a summary of the BTES Study.

4. Analyze the way goals are used to provide a framework for any educational program with which you are familiar. Select one or two educational goals related to the program and develop several goals which represent the department or program level. Suggest at least two course, unit, or topic goals related to each of your department or program goals.

5. Deepen your understanding of at least one major learning theory by reading appropriate references in the psychology of education. Generate a list of principles or guidelines that could be used by supporters of that theory to help guide the planning and operation of instructional programs.

Bibliography

Bellon, J. J., and E. C. Bellon. *Classroom Supervision and Instructional Improvement,* 2nd Edition. Dubuque: Kendall-Hunt Publishing Co., 1982.

Denham, Carolyn and Ann Lieberman. *Time to Learn.* Washington, D.C.: The National Institute of Education, 1980.

Good, Thomas L. and Jere E. Brophy. *Looking in Classrooms.* New York: Harper and Row Publishers, 1978.

Goodlad, John I. "What Goes On In Our Schools," *Educational Researcher.* Vol. 6, No. 3, March 1977, pp. 3–6.

Gronlund, Norman E. *Stating Behavioral Objectives for Classroom Use.* London: The MacMillan Co., 1978.

Popham, W. James. *Educational Evaluation.* Englewood Cliffs, N.J.: Prentice-Hall, Inc., 1975.

Worthen, Blaine R. and James K. Sanders. *Educational Evaluation: Theory and Practice.* Worthington, Ohio: Charles A. Jones Publishing Co., 1973.

Annotated Bibliography

Bellon, J. J., E. C. Bellon, and J. R. Handler. *Instructional Improvement: Principles and Processes.* Dubuque, Iowa: Kendall-Hunt Publishing Co., 1977. Identified are six important instructional areas which are crucial for improving student learning outcomes. An excellent resource for those interested in a systematic, cooperative approach to instructional improvement.

Bloom, Benjamin S. *Human Characteristics and School Learning.* New York: McGraw-Hill Book Company, 1976. The view that most students become very similar with regard to learning ability, rate of learning, and motivation for learning when provided with favorable learning conditions is presented. This theory is supported by research findings.

Chapter 7

Assessing Program Outcomes

Introduction

Measurement of program outcomes was for many years the most common form of curriculum evaluation. During the early decades of the twentieth century, standardized tests were the preferred form of measurement. They were virtually the only widely used evaluation tools. While these instruments are useful, they have limited value when a comprehensive analysis of the curriculum is desired. Standardized tests often do not relate directly to the local educational program. They also tend to have limited usefulness for assessing personal growth or social development.

As the development and evaluation field became more sophisticated, outcome evaluation was influenced by the work of Tyler and others. The major concern in relation to outcomes was no longer simply the measurement of results. Finding out whether stated goals had been achieved assumed greater importance. By focusing on the expected outcomes set forth in goal statements, evaluators were likely to select more relevant measurement instruments. However, the instruments failed in many cases to analyze important unintended results. These unexpected outcomes might have positive or negative effects on overall program success.

Curriculum evaluation experienced a tremendous surge during the late 1960's. This occurred primarily as a response to demands for accountability in the heavily funded federal programs of that era. The project evaluations conducted at that time were frequently outcome assessments, with little if any systematic attention to important organizational or process features. Pretest-posttest designs were often used to demonstrate successful achievement of program outcomes. Attitudes as well as cognitive outcomes were included in many designs, but instruments used to measure changes in attitudes frequently had questionable validity.

The development and evaluation design recommended in this book treats program outcomes differently from earlier measurement designs. Unlike these earlier approaches, the outcome phase is just one of several important dimensions studied. It is part of a dynamic process in which status information about program outcomes is made available for use in other phases of improvement. Further, the outcomes phase is not viewed as the end of development and evaluation activities. Except for short term special projects or programs that are to be terminated, findings concerning outcomes are used to stimulate further curriculum improvement.

Basic Concepts and Definitions

The definition of the term, outcomes, influences the strategies used in this phase of development and evaluation. As indicated earlier, outcome assessment has undergone several major changes through the years. It is important to define outcomes as more than measurable changes in learner knowledge or skills. Outcomes can be defined as the effects of a program on the participants and on the educational setting in which the program operates. This definition supports the activities generated by a comprehensive evaluation design. Implicit in the definition are several concepts which need to be reinforced. Outcomes are not just those things that happen to students, although these are certainly of primary importance. A program that is helping students achieve desired goals but causing excessive paperwork or morale problems for teachers cannot be judged a total success. Alternative ways of meeting the goals must be developed to prevent negative attitudes that may affect the entire curriculum. Similarly, administrators, other school personnel, and parents are affected by an educational program. Examining outcomes in relation to all clients, not just the students, is an important feature of the outcomes definition.

It is also important to recognize that this view of outcomes reduces the likelihood that all major program effects will be evident at a particular time. Several stages of curriculum outcomes need to be considered. First, the status study should reveal past and present outcomes and ways that they have been measured or identified. Status descriptions may indicate how outcome information is presently used by program planners.

Second, as a program is carried out, the development and evaluation process should generate data about interim outcomes. Periodic assessments help in judging progress toward the desired results. This enables corrective action to be taken if needed. Interim outcome assessment should take place on a scheduled basis that leads to the final summary evaluation. The final summation should provide a comprehensive analysis of all program outcomes.

Finally, some data should be gathered concerning long term program effects. This should include those effects that emerge after the outcome data have been summarized and assessed. By designing an ongoing development and evaluation process, a systematic follow up can be built into other data collection activities. Many important learning outcomes such as: application of known facts, synthesis of ideas and concepts, or strengthening of value systems are achieved over a long period of time. In order to measure learning achievement an ongoing evaluation program is needed.

Clearly, the variety of possible program effects requires attention over a period of time. A range of instruments is needed to gather appropriate long term outcome data. It is helpful to make use of both coarse grained and fine grained instruments to generate needed outcome data. Coarse grained instruments can be used for a relatively global portrayal of outcomes. They are designed to be convenient to administer and interpret. Fine grained instruments provide detailed inquiry into specific types of outcomes, often restricted to a particular skill or knowledge area. For example, a survey or interview may provide coarse grained data about the reading program while diagnostic tests may permit fine grained analysis of students' progress in reading comprehension.

Outcomes may also be studied through unobtrusive measures. Unobtrusive data collection is done without the direct involvement or even awareness of program participants. Attendance patterns, records of equipment utilization, or other indirect evidence can be helpful in assessing program results. However, this information is generally quite inferential. As a result, unobtrusive indicators may be subject to different interpretations. This may lead to difficulty in establishing relationships between outcomes and specific programs.

When planning strategies for the outcome phase, it should be expected that there will be varying degrees of inference and judgment. To many curriculum specialists, one of the most exciting trends in the field is a shift toward more extensive use of personal, qualitative data sources that are used to convey the essence of a program. While total reliance cannot be placed on highly subjective data for development and evaluation, recognition of the contribution made by these techniques is a promising step forward.

Propositions about Outcomes

When people think about the outcomes of educational programs, they tend to focus on pay-offs and products. While this way of thinking may be satisfactory for business and industry, it is not appropriate for curriculum evaluation. The propositions presented in this section reflect the unique role of educational organizations. Educational programs developed and evaluated by curriculum workers require different sets of conditions for success. Propositions that should be considered for curriculum outcome evaluation are:

Proposition A: Those responsible for planning and carrying out educational programs should view accountability for educational outcomes as an important influence in improvement efforts. Accountability should be regarded as beneficial to those involved in the operation of educational programs as well as to recipients of the services provided. It is true that educators have often reacted defensively to the demand for accountability. This has often been a reaction to the misuse of accountability for political purposes. However, sincere efforts must still be made to demonstrate that educators are willing to be held accountable for program outcomes. Reasonable, well planned steps must be taken to deliver on promised expectations. Accountability does not imply that every goal must be fully achieved by every student. It does not require that arbitrary standards based on testing programs should be used to evaluate teacher or administrator performance. When appropriately challenging goals are established not all of them will be met to the same degree, and some may not be achieved within a specific time period.

When systematic development and evaluation processes are used, program outcomes should reflect a natural relationship to stated goals. Since steps will have been taken during earlier phases to improve the goals, organization, and operation of the program, there should seldom be any unsuspected major deficiencies identified during outcome evaluation. Potential problems will generally have been attended to when they are first identified. Staff members will have been alerted to potential problems so that they can be corrected as soon as possible. This tends to make the work more satisfying and successful as staff members establish a pattern of regular progress toward achievement of their goals. A systematic approach to accountability helps clients feel that a conscientious effort to deliver high quality services is seen as a top priority.

Proposition B: Objectivity should be sought and maintained in assessing program outcomes. By the time the outcome phase of the development and evaluation process is reached, there has usually been a great deal of contact with program staff and clients. The evaluation team has often helped solve problems, clarify expectations, suggest ideas for organizing resources, observe classes, and so on. Such interactions are vital to a positive, improvement oriented development and evaluation approach. However, they may result in less objectivity when it is time to evaluate the results of program plans and activities.

Complete objectivity is seldom possible when human judgment and decision making are involved. Even if feasible, such extreme objectivity would probably lead to a very mechanistic process. However, it is important to take steps to maintain a reasonably high degree of objectivity at the outcome stage of curriculum evaluation.

There are several strategies for reducing the influence of evaluation bias or preconceptions. If an evaluation team has been involved in analyzing goals, organization, and operations, one or more new members can be added to the group. These individuals can join or substitute for selected team members to lend a fresh perspective to the overall review of program data. The new members should have the necessary background and skills to be productive in this role, but they should not be directly involved with the program being studied.

At times it is sufficient to put together a diverse team for the total evaluation process, relying on their differing backgrounds and professional interests to stimulate full discussion of all important issues. Establishing procedures and guidelines for data collection and anlaysis activities in advance can also increase the objectivity of outcome assessment. By maintaining awareness of the need to consider all the evidence and review both intended and unintended outcomes, personal preference or subjectivity can generally be kept in perspective.

Proposition C: Cost-benefit analysis and comparative evaluations should be used sparingly and with caution. It is natural in a cost conscious and efficiency oriented society for curriculum workers to borrow evaluation concepts from the business world. The idea of cost-benefit analysis is a business concept that has had moderate appeal for curriculum evaluation. The term seems to suggest sound accounting practices and careful fiscal management.

The notion of comparative evaluation, where the outcomes of one program are judged in relation to a new or established competitor, has also been urged as a model for curriculum assessment. One strategy is to identify a similar community and group of students currently using a comparable program. Test results or other data are gathered to determine which approach seems to yield better results. A different strategy is to try first one program and then another, under similar conditions, to compare how students perform in each case.

The limitations inherent in both cost-benefit analysis and comparative evaluation make their use highly questionable. To determine the actual costs and benefits of educational experiences seems to be a virtually impossible task. Judgments of worth or benefit are inseparable from basic value questions and should not be answered by formula or prescription. Some programs which serve few students and are quite costly may have considerable intrinsic worth or long term value. Special education programs, electronics or computer labs, physics classes, and foreign language offerings are just a few programs which might fall into this category. Outcomes of such programs should be assessed on the basis of both qualitative and quantitative criteria. Local beliefs and expectations must be carefully considered when evaluating such programs.

The rationale for urging caution in the use of comparative evaluation reflects a concern about what is often a pseudo-scientific approach. It is rather clear that the processes of development and evaluation are transportable from one setting to another. However, without adherence to sound research design principles, program results obtained in one setting cannot be assumed to apply elsewhere. Past and current practices in the local context are major influences when each program is planned, organized, and implemented. Decisions about curriculum outcomes are best interpreted in relation to their unique set of local conditions and influences. If comparative data are used, great care should be taken so that they do not unduly influence development and evaluation activities.

A Design for Outcome Analysis

Activities designed for the outcomes phase of development and evaluation should be consistent with the propositions set forth in this chapter. By carefully planning the outcome analysis, those responsible can efficiently use information gathered during prior evaluation activities. At the same time, appropriate new information should be acquired to help ensure a thorough, objective portrayal of results.

It may be helpful for the outcome analysis to include assistance from a statistician, measurement specialist, or other needed resource persons. As noted in Proposition B, adding new members to the evaluation team who have not been actively involved in the development and evaluation process will strengthen the outcome evaluation. These individuals can assist in identifying suitable criteria for judging program outcomes. They may be quite familiar with professional association guidelines and current research findings related to the curriculum. This information can be useful in conducting the analysis process. In addition, the views of these team members can lend increased objectivity to the outcome assessment.

As indicated earlier, the timing of outcome analysis activities is an important consideration. The design should include suitable attention to immediate results, short range outcomes, and if possible long term effects of the program. Major emphasis will in most cases need to be placed on outcomes that can be studied during the program and at a designated stopping point such as the end of a marking period, semester, or school year.

The status description of current outcomes should provide a good deal of information about past and present results. It should give a general indication about how program outcomes have been previously assessed, and what trends in learner performance have been identified. The status study may also reveal whether results of standardized testing or other activities are actually being used. The status information can serve as a valuable checkpoint and frame of reference for the outcome analysis.

Similarly, by the time the outcome analysis is conducted, detailed information about program operations should be available. This information is often valuable in studying interim outcomes or progressive steps toward goal achievement. Performance on daily classwork, unit tests, and other ongoing measures will indicate whether student progress has been consistent or sporadic. Observation data can also be reviewed for indications of program effectiveness.

It may be helpful to allocate some of the resources available for outcome analysis to short range follow up activities. These activities would generally occur within six months to a year of the first assessment of outcomes. Depending upon the program, some longer range follow up activities may be important. If the program has been operating for several years, former students can provide helpful information. Their experiences cannot be assumed to have been identical to those of current students, but their views can supplement other data sources.

Another important consideration in planning the outcome analysis is the range of results to be assessed. It is crucial to analyze the extent to which stated goals have been achieved. Unanticipated outcomes must also be examined so that the overall impact of the program is known. Indicators of effects on the students served, their peers and teachers, and other persons or events need to be obtained. A well planned and comprehensive data collection strategy is necessary if the important outcome questions are to be addressed.

In designing the strategy for data collection, steps must be taken to obtain adequate information for sound decision making. However, it is unwise to engage in excessive testing or other forms of measurement. The importance of academic learning time or opportunity to learn has been emphasized in recent classroom research. The amount of learning time spent on data collection should be restricted to essential measurement activities.

There are several steps that can be taken to strike the appropriate balance between efficiency and completeness in data collection. For the development and evaluation process it may be very helpful to use sampling techniques to distribute measurement contacts. For example, all students may not need to complete every test or survey instrument. Sample groups can be selected to reduce the total time each student is involved in these activities. Similarly, a lengthy test with subtests may not have to be given intact, but can often be parceled out to randomly chosen groups. Naturally, the tradeoffs involved in any time and expense saving strategies must be carefully weighed by the evaluation team. However, every attempt should be made to make the outcome analysis as smooth and nondisruptive as possible.

It is essential to select or develop high quality tools for data collection. While educational goals do not need to be measured directly nor within a particular time frame, it is appropriate to measure objectives. Goals serve as direction giving statements of purpose or intent. Objectives provide indicators that satisfactory progress toward goal attainment is being made. When all objectives are assessed, it is possible to determine whether or not the goals of the program have been achieved to a satisfactory degree.

There are a large number of instruments available for measuring all types of outcomes. Achievement, personality, attitudes, psychomotor skills, and many other areas can be studied through a wide variety of techniques. If tests, rating scales, inventories, or alternative published instruments are sought, references such as the *Mental Measurements Yearbook* (1978) or *Tests in Print* (1974) can be consulted for specific examples. Specialists may also be able to give helpful advice in choosing appropriate instruments. Considerations in test selection include: validity, reliability, scoring and administration factors, cost, and format in which results are reported. Some types of instruments, such as personality profiles or rating scales, have inherent limitations that should also be considered.

Informal techniques can be a very useful supplement to more formal measurement. Discussions with students or teachers often provide valuable data. Samples of student work, results of teacher made tests, observation of creative performances or skill demonstrations, and similar techniques may all play a role in the data collection for outcome analysis. Informal strategies can also help determine the extent to which students, teachers, parents and administrators receive accurate and useful information about a program and its outcomes.

Similarly, unobtrusive indicators, gained without specific involvement of students or others, can be informative. Students who attend classes regularly, sign up for further experiences of the same type, check out library resources related to the program, and complete assigned tasks may be judged to have positive feelings toward the experiences being provided. These can be seen only as indicators and must be used with great care. However, a pattern which is fairly consistent and widespread would probably represent an accurate portrayal of student attitudes. Indirect indicators can also be used to study effects on teachers, parents, or other groups. Changes that occur in related programs, in the general climate of the school or system, or in interpersonal relationships might appropriately be studied through informal and indirect means. Sudden increases or declines in discipline problems, major shifts in course requests or enrollments, and marked changes in parent-school contacts are examples of possible spinoff effects worth investigating.

The value of timely, appropriate collection of outcome data has been stressed. A further consideration in the design for outcome analysis concerns the criteria for judging success. Some thought should be given before information is gathered to the type of criteria or judgment standards which will be used. Specific cutoff scores or quantitative standards are not necessary or even appropriate in many cases. However, there are many people who advocate their use. Decisions must be made about appropriate sources of criteria such as professional organizations, leading authorities, and state or national guidelines. It is also important to consider whose input should be obtained in deciding upon criteria. The extent to which formal criteria are needed will vary with the program being studied. In most improvement efforts, clear and pertinent evaluation criteria are regarded as a distinct asset.

An outcome analysis organized around the features described in this section should help answer a number of important questions. Obtaining information about these concerns should be seen as a major step toward long term curriculum improvement. Questions that can be helpful for outcome analysis include:

1. Have all program goals been satisfactorily achieved?
2. Were the unintended outcomes found to be positive?
3. Has appropriate use been made of information from prior development and evaluation phases?
4. Have sound measurement techniques and high quality instruments been used to collect data about outcomes?
5. Does a process exist for systematically using outcome information for program improvement?

Responses to questions such as these can enable the development and evaluation team to make recommendations with considerable confidence. The questions also help in establishing the conditions needed for continuing program improvement.

Relationship to Other Development and Evaluation Approaches

The outcome phase of the systematic development and evaluation process described in this chapter directs attention to program goal achievement. An interest in unanticipated effects has also been expressed. Approaches that focus exclusively on goals are not considered adequate. Similarly, many problems have surfaced in attempts to assess outcomes without adequately considering goals, organization, operations, and pervasive influences. Except for limited purposes, it is hard to justify any curriculum improvement process that is not comprehensive.

In Stake's evaluation framework, a similar position is apparent. His outcome stage follows an assessment of antecedent conditions and actual program transactions. The relationships between antecendents, transactions, and outcomes are studied to be sure they reflect sound overall planning. Judgment is used in determining, through a broad range of qualitative and quantitative outcome indicators, how well intended results have been realized. A check is often made to see that unintended effects do not counteract the intended results. Standards or judgment criteria also play a role in Stake's approach.

There has been some debate through the years on the appropriate role of intrinsic and extrinsic criteria. Intrinsic criteria represent features or characteristics of a program which are valued for their own sake. Accreditation activities often rely heavily on intrinsic criteria such as the size of the library collection, variety of courses offered, and qualifications of staff members. When extrinsic criteria are used, there is a greater concern for payoffs or effects on students or other clients. Scriven used the term payoff evaluation to describe a process focusing solely on clearcut program effects. Attention to both types of criteria provides the best basis for curriculum improvement.

The well known frameworks proposed by Stufflebeam, Alkin, and Provus include an outcome oriented phase. In Stufflebeam's CIPP model this phase is called Product Evaluation and the focus is on whether or not objectives have been achieved. The Provus discrepancy model includes a Product stage and follows it with a phase designated Program Comparison. This framework explicitly incorporates a comparative analysis in which cost-benefit relationships are studied. As pointed out earlier, it is generally not productive to build these dimensions into the development and evaluation process, although they may be useful in particular situations.

A unique approach suggested by Scriven and tested in several different contexts is the goal free evaluation process. As conceived by Scriven, various aspects of program functioning would be studied without prior knowledge of actual program goals. This approach was proposed as a way to prevent the goals from acting as blinders or perceptual screens that might cause an evaluator to overlook important side effects or unintended outcomes. Biases such as these should be controlled as much as possible. By systematically designing the outcome analysis process to include measures of unanticipated as well as expected outcomes a satisfactory degree of objectivity and accuracy can usually be achieved.

Before concluding this discussion of outcome evaluation, it may be well to briefly mention two terms which have been extensively used in recent years: formative and summative evaluation. Scriven suggested these terms in the late 1960's to distinguish two types of evaluation activities. Those activities which sought to make improvements while a program was being planned or implemented were called formative. Evaluation activities leading to decisions to continue, terminate, or modify a completed program were referred to as summative.

Since these terms became popular they have frequently been misused. Summative evaluation has often been treated as a synonym for outcome evaluation or assumed to apply only to fully completed programs. Most educational programs are in fact ongoing, with decisions to terminate being made very infrequently. Formative evaluation activities provide feedback for program refinement. They seem to be needed most often in education. However, it is still important to periodically engage in a summative review of program expectations and outcomes. This helps program staff members improve their long range planning and assess overall results.

The systematic approach to development and evaluation that has been proposed can serve either formative or summative functions. The process can be applied as readily to a program being tried for the first time or one which is being reviewed after years of operation. Early application of the development and evaluation process will help strengthen the program initially and identify minor weaknesses before they become serious. However, a summative assessment of goals, organization, operations, and outcomes can also be very worthwhile over a period of time. The information from a summative assessment can be most helpful in developing ongoing school improvement programs. In the following chapter, leadership strategies are described that are essential when programs are to be developed or changed.

Development and Renewal Activities

1. Identify the types of outcome data that have been gathered for an educational program evaluation with which you are familiar. Using appropriate measurement references or other resources, develop a list of several specific alternatives for obtaining the same types of data. Compare these with the strategies that were used and develop recommendations that would improve the original evaluation.

2. A large number of techniques are available for obtaining outcome information. Several have been mentioned in the chapter. These techniques include: standardized tests, personality inventories, attitude scales, observation instruments, and questionnaires. Select one or more techniques about which you would like to have more information. Become more familiar with each through reading, examining samples, and discussing important features with colleagues or other appropriate persons. Propose a set of guidelines that can be helpful to curriculum workers in choosing a suitable data collection technique.

3. There has recently been a good deal of attention focused on the relative advantages and disadvantages of criterion referenced and norm referenced measurement. A normative measure is one that reports scores in relation to the performance of a selected "norm group" that was administered the instrument. A criterion referenced measure in designed to indicate the extent to which particular objectives or classes of behaviors have been acquired. Become better acquainted with the current debate about these techniques by reading appropriate articles in recent publications. In addition, reports of a highly publicized adversary evaluation hearing on minimum competency testing held in Washington, D.C. during the summer of 1981 would be helpful in understanding the issues surrounding test utilization (Thurston and House, 1981).

Bibliography

Buros, Oscar, ed. *Mental Measurements Yearbook, 8th edition.* Highland Park, N.J.: Gryphon Press, 1978.
———. *Tests in Print—Two: An Index to Tests, Test Reviews and the Literature on Specific Tests.* Highland Park, N.J.: Gryphon Press, 1974.
Popham, W. James. *Educational Evaluation.* Englewood Cliffs, N.J.: Prentice-Hall, Inc., 1975.
Thurston, Paul and Ernest R. House. "The NIE Adversary Hearing on Minimum Competency Testing," *Phi Delta Kappan.* Vol. 63, No. 2, October 1981, pp. 87–89.
Tyler, Ralph W. *Basic Principles of Curriculum and Instruction.* Chicago: University of Chicago Press, 1949.
Worthen, Blaine R. and James K. Sanders. *Educational Evaluation: Theory and Practice.* Worthington, Ohio: Charles A. Jones Publishing Co., 1973.

Chapter 8

Leadership for Curriculum Development and Evaluation

Introduction

Throughout this book the advantages of a comprehensive development and evaluation process have been presented and discussed. When programs are regularly examined in terms of their goals, organization, operations, and outcomes, improvements can generally be effectively accomplished. However, it would be naive to assume that a sound development and evaluation strategy can itself ensure successful program results. Conditions must be present which increase the probability that intended strategies will be accepted by those whose involvement is crucial to long term success. These conditions are largely a function of the leadership present in the schools.

Although much has been written about leadership styles and behaviors, a good deal less attention has been paid to the implications of these findings for program improvement. The principles and practices discussed in earlier chapters suggest a number of specific conditions that support curriculum change efforts. The growing body of evidence on the importance of principals' instructional leadership roles also provides useful information for those seeking to establish a success oriented context for curriculum activity. Studies by the Rand Corporation (1975) and other research groups suggest that the building principal may be the key person for overall school effectiveness. Examining the behavior patterns of the most successful school leaders has yielded several major findings concerning their interpersonal and task related functioning. These and other data sources form the basis of the following discussion about the leadership conditions essential to lasting curriculum improvement.

As important as these conditions are in general, they take on even greater significance in situations characterized by change or uncertainty. Many school systems today are faced with substantial declines in funding and enrollment. These declines can be taken as a signal for cutbacks and retrenchment. They can also be seen as an opportunity to develop higher quality, more effective programs. By paying attention to leadership conditions in the local situation, curriculum workers can help shape rather than just react to external and internal influences. A direct, forward looking approach to leadership and curriculum change has long term benefits for the overall functioning of the entire school system.

Basic Concepts and Definitions

The study of leadership has been approached in many different ways through the years. Early writers focused on the traits that seemed to characterize effective leaders. Subsequent theorists have proposed various explanations about how leaders function in groups and complex organizations. Classification systems can be found that deal primarily with leadership styles but place little emphasis on the setting or situation.

Important contributions have recently been made by James MacGregor Burns (1978) to the analysis of leadership behavior. His distinction between transactional and transformational leadership is especially pertinent in defining what leaders do. Transactional leaders engage in activities which help ensure that the current goals of the organization are achieved. This form of leadership is a process of interaction and exchange through which people are motivated to work toward goals established or accepted by the leader. In transformational leadership, there is a more dynamic approach to the goals or purposes sought and to the processes through which goals are met. The transformational leader helps members of the organization redefine and clarify their goals, encouraging them to strive for renewed professional and personal achievement. Support is then provided by the leader in various ways as people begin to move in new directions and accept new challenges.

There is a place in educational organizations for both types of leaders. Transactional leaders can be very effective in guiding programs that are fairly stable in terms of expectations and performance. They do more than simply manage or administer these programs. Their roles may call for high levels of interpersonal and motivational skills. However, it is the transformational concept of leadership that is needed when program improvement is sought, particularly on a large scale. The transformational leader helps create an atmosphere where growth and change are valued not feared. People interacting with a transformational leader seem to gain from this association a greater ability and willingness to make commitments that involve risks or uncertainties. Clearly these attitudes help establish conditions for productive curriculum activity.

An important concept for understanding leadership and its effects is the delineation of ascribed versus natural or informal leadership. Ascribed leaders occupy positions in the organization that explicitly specify some designated leadership responsibilities. Their positions place them in charge of programs and personnel, either temporarily or on an ongoing basis. Ascribed leaders can be identified by their assigned roles and functions in the organization.

An analysis of leadership that fails to go beyond the designated leaders cannot accurately portray the real state of affairs in the organization. Informal leadership can be as influential as the formal leadership in an organization. The leadership picture may bear little resemblance to the actual work situation depicted on an organizational chart. While this may not be the desired situation, it is certainly one that needs to be recognized by those who seek to improve the curriculum. In some schools one or more teachers may be the real leaders. Their leadership roles may or may not be viewed positively, but they definitely need to be taken into account in planning development and evaluation activities.

A concept that merits more attention by curriculum workers is the notion that every teacher is a highly influential leader. Teachers are important leaders of their students and often their peers. They may not be used to thinking of themselves in this light, but their leadership influence can be very powerful. Leadership can, in fact, be found and should be cultivated at all levels of the organization. When more people feel and act in ways that characterize effective leaders, the positive effects will be felt throughout the system.

The benefits of multi-level leadership are best achieved when there is unity of purpose. It is not functional to have each staff member pursuing individual goals without regard for common purposes. Agreed upon goals are a key element of effective leadership. In addition to the educational goals discussed at length in Chapter 4, organizational goals should be established and reviewed regularly by personnel at all levels. All staff members should be able to show a relationship between the goals they would like to work toward as individuals and the general direction or expectations that have been established for the total system. Overall organizational goals should be based on the best thinking of all major groups in the organization so that all participants will make a commitment to achieving the high priority goals. For example, an organizational goal may deal with establishing systematic program evaluation processes. Each staff member would be expected to work toward this important goal in appropriate ways. Leadership would need to be provided to generate and sustain high levels of commitment and involvement in this crucial area. Without effective leadership, such worthwhile goals are often established with a fanfare but are soon neglected and never receive any real attention.

Propositions about Leadership for Curriculum Improvement

In this section, several propositions are discussed which can help ensure that important goals do receive the attention needed for successful implementation. The ideas set forth in the propositions can provide a helpful starting point for strengthening local curriculum leadership. Their relationship to the principles supported throughout this book should be evident. They represent some of the most important ways one can establish the conditions for successful curriculum development and evaluation in the local setting.

A. **Effective leaders should model the behaviors they desire in others.** It has been shown that modeling is one of the most powerful and influential teaching techniques. At the classroom level, modeling involves clear, explicit demonstrations of the behaviors expected of students. In a leadership context, modeling is also a process of demonstrating through consistent words and actions the behaviors sought within the organization.

When leaders take steps to demonstrate that they themselves do the things they expect of others, organizational goals are far more likely to be realized. These individuals serve as positive models of desired performance. They make it clear that they are doing more than just giving lip service to the ideas they espouse. Such leaders have recognized how unrealistic it is to expect staff members to make a commitment to activities that are said to be important but are seldom actually practiced.

Unfortunately, examples are abundant where leaders have tried to initiate important changes through words alone, with no accompanying action. For example, it has been typical to institute evaluation programs at the classroom or building level. Leaders at higher organizational levels have often proclaimed the importance of evaluation while offering little evidence of top-down evaluation activities starting with their own positions. Similar patterns have been evident in relation to goal setting, renewal, and other leadership responsibilities.

Because of the problems associated with ineffective leadership, there seems to be a growing awareness of the need for demonstrated commitment to personal and organizational improvement. Leaders who have used modeling to set a pattern for desired performance attest to the value of this approach. The benefits extend not only to the organization and its members, but to the leaders themselves. They tend to gain a much deeper understanding of their own reactions or abilities as well as those of others. These insights can have substantial payoff in improving many different aspects of the leadership roles within the organization.

B. **Leadership is most successful when people are stimulated to pursue new goals for themselves and the organization.** Curriculum and instruction leaders who are able to instill a clear sense of purpose and direction in those with whom they work have established an attitude that leads to success. People who experience this feeling of movement toward some understood and accepted outcomes are positively motivated to seek continued progress. The knowledge that personal efforts are directed toward goal attainment is most reinforcing when the goals are seen as important. Personal involvement in setting or adopting the goals lends added strength to these motivational effects.

Leaders of educational organizations, particularly in a period of declining resources and low levels of faculty turnover, must be especially sensitive to the problems of stagnation and complacency. It is not unusual to find school systems that continue to bask in past achievements. They may fail to recognize that in a period of rapid change and expanding knowledge, the failure to grow and improve virtually guarantees that programs will show signs of deterioration. In some school systems, low expectations have been allowed to become entrenched and interfere with productive growth. Persons working in these systems tend to dwell on the reasons why changes are doomed to failure. Thinking backward more often than forward, these individuals use past experiences to demonstrate the obstacles to success. Unfortunately, such negative expectations are likely to be self-fulfilling as more and more reasons are found to avoid new commitments.

When leaders recognize the dangers inherent in regressive situations and are willing to take steps to establish more desirable patterns, great strides can be made. Leaders who believe that people want to feel competent and be seen by others as competent in their work have an added edge. These positive assumptions about human behavior help leaders trust others, build on current strengths, and persevere when improvement comes slowly.

As leaders encourage members of the organization to set new goals and strive for continued growth, they can play a valuable role by providing feedback and support. Their feedback can aid in screening feasible, important goals from those that would be less important. The resources and moral support that leaders provide can also contribute greatly to individual success. Both elements are important in establishing the conditions for personal and professional success within the educational organization.

C. **It is not possible to teach people to become leaders, but skills and processes can be learned which help develop potential leadership talent.** Training programs for leadership have been popular and continue to attract a number of hopeful participants. However, there has not been convincing evidence that leadership ability can be created through training experiences. This does not mean that leadership effectiveness cannot be improved.

Although there are no easy paths to acquiring leadership talent, it has been repeatedly demonstrated that potential leaders can take steps to improve their likelihood of success. They can analyze and refine their skills in several critical areas found to be strongly associated with leadership effectiveness. These include: planning, decision making, communication, and interpersonal functioning. Individuals able to understand and apply several different strategies in each of these crucial areas can respond positively and appropriately to many diverse situations. Related to these essential process skills are current leadership concerns such as time management and human resource development. By engaging in ongoing staff development activities, individuals in any position can increase their potential success as educational leaders.

It is also becoming apparent that effective leadership requires a commitment to intellectual and physical renewal as well as growth in interpersonal relationships and other process skills. Aspy and Roebuck (1977) found positive correlations between the levels of fitness and interpersonal functioning demonstrated by principals and their teachers. Gardner (1974) has written of the need for personal renewal activities that include systematic steps to encourage growth in intellectual, emotional, physical, and other realms of human activity. These important findings help confirm the belief that effective leadership requires high levels of energy. Not everyone who develops increased energy will become a successful leader, but few people can be truly effective leaders if they lack the intellectual, emotional, and physical stamina to meet the demands and challenges that face most leaders.

Leadership Implications in the Design for Improvement

Adopting a planned, comprehensive approach to curriculum development and evaluation is an important and far reaching decision. The design for improvement that has been presented in this book can be most effectively implemented when favorable leadership conditions are present. Establishing and maintaining these desired conditions can be a challenging process. It is certainly worthwhile if the full benefits of ongoing development and evaluation activities are to be realized. The following subsections focus on strengthening local leadership to promote curriculum improvement. Implications are presented in three major areas: staff development, personnel evaluation, and utilization of development and evaluation findings.

Before turning to these important topics, several variables should be noted that are influential in all three areas. Those concerned with the quality of leadership conditions must pay attention to people, tasks, information, and the context for change. The characteristics of people in the organization and the ways that these individuals interact with each other can have a significant impact on virtually any leadership situation. Interpersonal skills of the leaders and others must be a concern if the development and evaluation process is to function most effectively. When satisfactory working relationships have not been established within the organization, leaders must take steps to strengthen this area so that development and evaluation activities can proceed smoothly.

As the development and evaluation activities take place, members of the organization will be expected to accomplish a number of specified tasks. Some will be complex and time consuming, while others are likely to be quite simple. Similarly, development and evaluation tasks can be expected to vary in the degree to which they: require cooperative effort, generate support or resistance with the organization, and represent structured or loosely defined activities. Leaders must make appropriate decisions about matching people with tasks to increase the chances of success in the total improvement program.

One of the variables that should have an influence on leadership decisions is the attitude toward change prevalent within the organization. While some educational organizations react well to change and regularly review and modify their curricula, other organizations reflect negative, change resistant attitudes. Members of the resistant organizations often feel that too many changes have been made and not sustained. They may also feel pressured to become involved in changes not perceived as meaningful or worthwhile. Successful leaders need to be aware of staff members' attitudes toward change. They must develop strategies for encouraging positive attitudes about improvement.

One additional variable warrants comment in this discussion. The management of information is a process that has only recently begun to be acknowledged as a major influence on development and evaluation activities. When the information gathered is insufficient or fails to address the most important concerns for program improvement, satisfactory results are unlikely. With the computer technology available today, the problem of generating excess information is at least as severe as having insufficient data. If the development and evaluation process produces data that are not readily interpretable by decision makers, critical information may be misused. Sound techniques for managing development and evaluation information are emerging as important requirements for those giving leadership to curriculum improvement programs.

Implications Concerning Staff Development

The adoption of a systematic approach to curriculum development and evaluation has a number of important implications for staff development. The idea of refining and strengthening staff performance through appropriate developmental experiences is certainly not new. However, these experiences have often been sporadic and have usually been provided only for teachers. Educational leaders in many systems are coming to accept the need for appropriate staff development at all levels of the organization. For example, those in key leadership positions within the organization can profit from activities that help strengthen their interpersonal or decision making skills. By enhancing these skills, leaders' abilities to carry out crucial development and evaluation responsibilities can also be improved.

In order to be most effective, staff development activities for all members of the organization must be related to personal improvement needs. When the development and evaluation process reveals individual or group needs related to instruction, goal setting, planning, organization, or other areas, steps should be taken to provide appropriate support. Although it has been typical to resort to workshops as the typical staff development format, there are numerous other options that can be beneficial to the participants. These include small group skill sessions, individual readings in specially selected materials, observation of colleagues, and analysis of performance using individual video or audiotapes. When staff development experiences are data based and tailored as closely as possible to the person and the situation, it is very likely that the improvement goals will be achieved.

As leaders initiate this personalized approach to staff development, the importance of the total improvement process will generally be more widely recognized. Staff development activities can ensure that all personnel are involved in some meaningful way in program improvement. These activities can reinforce the understanding that staff members' instructional and leadership skills must be constantly refined to better implement the curriculum, just as the curriculum itself must change in response to identified learner needs. Both types of changes require the kind of responsive support system that a well planned staff development program can provide.

Implications for Personnel Evaluation

Effective leaders are typically found to operate according to a consistent set of personal beliefs and assumptions. Their actions can generally be analyzed across time to reveal a fairly clear pattern of behavior in similar types of situations. It is important that the various major functions of the total organization also reflect a basic consistency and coherence.

The approach taken to staff development should mesh well with the curriculum development and evaluation process being used. Both programs should emphasize systematic improvement based on regular feedback and a high level of staff participation. A staff development program that emphasizes personalized growth experiences and builds on identified needs should be linked to a personnel evaluation process that provides the necessary data and also focuses on growth and improvement.

In order to fit well with the curriculum improvement approach presented in this book, the personnel evaluation process must demonstrate that there is an emphasis on positive change and improvement. It should be designed to yield objective data about performance. The process for gathering this information should be compatible with the assumptions about cooperation and collegiality that have been highlighted previously.

When these common elements are not present, it is much more difficult for leaders to be effective in personnel evaluation activities. There are many benefits that can be derived when development and evaluation processes truly function as complementary activities for programs and personnel. Staff members need to feel that their efforts to improve the curriculum and instructional program are recognized and rewarded. They should not be made to feel that their work is being assessed on unrelated criteria, through wholly subjective means, or with punitive motives. Those in designated leadership positions should also be evaluated using processes that are compatible with the overall improvement approach. Important goals for educational and organizational growth need to be reflected in evaluation instruments and procedures used at all levels of the system. When steps are taken to reinforce this consistency, a more effective, efficient, and successful educational program will result.

Implications for Utilization of Results

One of the issues currently receiving attention by specialists in educational evaluation is the disappointing level of follow up action. Many educational leaders are dismayed by the uneven utilization of findings published in evaluation reports. They are worried about credibility when the public remains largely unaware of the positive steps being taken to assess and improve educational programs.

When school systems adopt an ongoing process of development and evaluation, there are several factors that help avoid this poor utilization of information. The status study begins to identify concerns, perceptions, and other background information important to the local setting. Community influences and pressures from various levels are also probed, so that development and evaluation procedures can be designed to respond in a productive manner. This attention to contextual factors continues throughout the process, as feedback from appropriate groups and individuals is sought at every stage. In addition to gathering information, the process provides for regular reports to appropriate persons about interim findings and recommendations. An emphasis on clear, accurate, and timely communication is an essential feature of this systematic improvement approach.

To further ensure that results of curriculum improvement activities are widely understood and have the best chance of stimulating needed changes, there are additional steps that should be taken. Reports must be written in a style that is clear and factual, with nonprint media used to emphasize important information. These reports should be issued regularly to appropriate groups so that awareness and interest levels can be maintained. Problems or weaknesses should be dealt with honestly in all reports and materials. When development and evaluation function as ongoing processes, it becomes much easier for reports of improvement needs to be accompanied by thoughtful plans for taking corrective action.

Leaders who become skillful in managing and communicating information about program improvement activities can generate substantial benefits. Support and enthusiasm can be developed by creating a genuine sense of teamwork and involvement. It is important to keep a balanced perspective and avoid promises that cannot possibly be met. Effective leaders find that they can counter negativism and pessimism by keeping all participants informed about changes and improvements being made. In their interactions with others, leaders should recognize that when changes are being made some conflict will naturally arise. Rather than suppressing or ignoring this inevitable conflict, they need to make plans to manage it openly and directly. They must also help staff members learn strategies that will be personally useful in managing future conflict situations.

Investing time and energy to develop strengths and build for the future seems in many ways to characterize a sound leadership approach. These priorities are highly compatible with the development and evaluation design presented in this book. Curriculum improvement should generate information about the past and present that can be systematically analyzed and lead to plans for future action. New goals may emerge from development and evaluation activities, requiring adjustments in other areas of program functioning. Effective leaders should take an active and energetic role in gaining support for new educational goals. They should view the development and evaluation process as one that, when properly installed, can be managed and monitored by the staff. Effective leaders are not hesitant to entrust important tasks to others, for they also know that appropriate staff development can be used to help ensure successful performance. By taking a gradual, developmental approach to change and growth, more people can understand and share in the process of developing a stronger curriculum. Both the process itself and any products or improvements generated are important to an effective, renewing and vital educational program.

Development and Renewal Activities

1. For a more thorough discussion of leadership, personnel evaluation, and related processes of instructional supervision, read appropriate chapters of *Classroom Supervision and Instructional Supervision,* 2nd edition, by Bellon and Bellon (Kendall/Hunt, 1982). Use the reference lists in each chapter to begin a regular program of personal readings in these important areas.

2. Analyze the leadership assumptions and practices that characterize an educational program you are familiar with. Focus on two or three key improvement needs that are identified by your analysis. Use the ideas presented in Chapter 8 to develop recommendations for strengthening the identified areas of concern. Suggest ways that local personnel could effectively communicate your findings and recommendations to various staff and client groups.

3. Develop a personal leadership assessment to help in understanding and strengthening your own skills. Use a position description, if one is available, and list the primary responsibilities or activities which require that you function in a leadership capacity. Analyze the ways that you typically handle various situations associated with these areas. Use the results of your analysis to identify leadership skills you feel fairly confident about, those which you'd like to strengthen, and those that may require further information if you are to assess your performance. Working alone or with a colleague, develop a plan that includes steps you can take to increase your leadership effectiveness.

Bibliography

Aspy, David N. and Flora N. Roebuck. *Kids Don't Learn From People They Don't Like.* Amherst, Mass.: Human Resource Development Press, Inc., 1977.

Bellon J. J., and E. C. Bellon. *Classroom Supervision and Instructional Improvement,* 2nd Edition. Dubuque: Kendall-Hunt Publishing Co., 1982.

Berman, Paul and Milbrey McLaughlin. *Federal Programs Supporting Educational Change: The Findings in Review.* R-1589/4-HEW, The Rand Corporation, April, 1975.

Burns, MacGregor James. *Leadership.* New York: Harper and Row, Publishers, 1978.

Gardner, John W. *Self-Renewal.* New York: Harper and Row Publishers, 1974.